Praise for
Point of View

"Elisabeth has captivated me—as she has most of America—from the beginning of her public life on *Survivor,* through her days on *The View,* and in her classy, intelligent presence on Fox & Friends. While this book chronicles details and events throughout her life, including those public forums, the thread of her faith and her commitment to Christ through all of those seasons inspires me like crazy."

   —SANDRA STANLEY, North Point Ministries, speaker and author

"Having it all may be impossible, but having most everything is only possible by living your faith as part of your journey. Elisabeth tells us how she does it—and so well."

   —DANA PERINO, White House press secretary to George W.
   Bush and host on Fox News

"Reading *Point of View* is like sitting down for a nice long coffee date with a good and gracious friend. Elisabeth is the real deal—full of passion, love, humility, strength, and a wholehearted love for God and people. In *Point of View,* Elisabeth takes the simple and not-so-simple happenings of everyday life and points us to the greater truths God has for us. She inspires with her triumphs, encourages with her life lessons, and gives grace for her failures and for our own."

   —KORIE ROBERTSON, A&E's *Duck Dynasty* and author of *Strong
   and Kind: Raising Kids of Character*

"Passionate and humble, sharp and inquisitive, capable and filled with childlike wonder, serious in her faith and as kindhearted as they come,

Elisabeth has this way of also bringing out the best in *us*. I'm confident that sitting with her as you read this lovely life-giving reflection will have the same effect on you."

—Scott Sauls, senior pastor of Christ Presbyterian Church in
Nashville, Tennessee, and author of *Befriend* and *Irresistible Faith*

"Refreshingly vulnerable and rich in honesty, Elisabeth Hasselbeck's *Point of View* carries a powerful message that reprioritizes the great truth: He calls, He equips, He never leaves."

—Roma Downey, actress, producer, and author

"Elisabeth exudes authentic joy, grace, and a spirit of humility. One conversation and you immediately feel genuine sisterhood from her. This book is much the same—full of wisdom and life lessons from a trusted friend. It will speak to you no matter where you are in your journey."

—Natalie Grant, Grammy-nominated singer and songwriter

"With captivating storytelling and priceless wisdom, Elisabeth extends a warm and generous invitation into the fascinating life she's lived and the God she loves. Her genuine desire to wholeheartedly love and serve the people God puts in her path will inspire you to passionately pursue a grace-full point of view in your own relationships."

—Jeannie Cunnion, author of *Mom Set Free*

"I have been blessed to know Elisabeth since she first arrived in New York City to work on *The View*. We have talked honestly together, prayed earnestly together, and cried vulnerably together. To know her is to love her. Her view will inspire you to trust for God's best in your life, to look each morning to His light to guide your way, and to stay joyfully on the unique

vulnerability, transparency, and most of all, dependence on her creator. She shows us how to make the absolute most of every single opportunity but is also humble enough to accept when God is gently guiding her into an entirely different realm of life. Thank you, Elisabeth, for encouraging us to go full force after our dreams, all while staying in His will."

—MISSY ROBERTSON, star of A&E's *Duck Dynasty* and *New York Times* best-selling author

"In *Point of View,* you'll discover the inspiring heart behind the life of Elisabeth Hasselbeck. What you'll also find is an uncommon perspective that's hopeful, faith filled, and gracious. It's a must-read for all!"

—COURTNEY DEFEO, author of *In This House, We Will Giggle* and founder of TreasuredGirlz.com

"One of the hardest battles to win is learning to respect others' opinions without being personally crippled by those who come against you. Elisabeth has written a much-needed message about this, woven throughout her fascinating story. In a world that sometimes begs us to do the total opposite, *Point of View* is a great resource that will help us process having a godly perspective."

—LYSA TERKEURST, *New York Times* best-selling author and president of Proverbs 31 Ministries path He has for you. In *Point of View,* you will learn to live, love, and leave well."

—Kathie Lee Gifford, co-host of *Today's* fourth hour

"Elisabeth has taught me how to be a better friend, mom, daughter, sister, leader, and follower of Jesus. Through this book and her life stories and practical advice, she will teach you the same!"

—Karris Hudson, vice president of Danita's Children

"As much as I loved reading the behind-the-scenes stories and insight from Elisabeth's life in the spotlight, what I loved most about *Point of View* is its challenge to trust God when I don't understand my circumstances, to be present and purposeful with my family, and to love people—even those I disagree with—in spirit and in action. Her book feels like a hug from an old friend, advice from a wise counselor, and a gentle push from a sister. Elisabeth's honesty about the highs and lows of life as a working mom left me encouraged and motivated to make some hard choices and love the season I'm in."

—Samantha Ponder, ESPN *Sunday NFL Countdown* host

"We all know Elisabeth to be a spirited fighter! *Point of View* unveils the source of the strength in her journey, inviting you into the wisdom and the life that has shaped her at every turn. You will be inspired and renewed to step into your story with a new fire."

—Chris Tomlin and Lauren Tomlin, songwriter
      and worship leaders

"God has given Elisabeth this platform to share many of her stori the rest of us can be inspired by her dreams, courage, endurance, ten

ELISABETH HASSELBECK

with BETH CLARK

POINT OF VIEW

**A Fresh Look at
Work, Faith, and Freedom**

Foreword by CANDACE CAMERON BURE

WATERBROOK

POINT OF VIEW

Hardcover ISBN 978-0-525-65276-2
eBook ISBN 978-0-525-65277-9

Printed in the United States of America
2019—First Edition

10 9 8 7 6 5 4 3 2 1

To my husband, Tim, and our children,
Grace, Taylor, and Isaiah. I love how we love.

So from now on we regard no one from a worldly point of view. Though we once regarded Christ in this way, we do so no longer.

—2 Corinthians 5:16

Contents

Foreword

Learning from Those Who Go Before Us

Along with millions of other viewers, I watched a cute unknown shoe designer—with her petite frame and blond hair—walk, talk, and struggle her way through television's *Survivor.* I watched in awe that such a little thing had a presence that was so bold. I loved that she didn't back down and was in it to win it, but not from a backstabbing, I-don't-care-about-anyone-but-myself mentality. There was something different about her.

I then watched this reality show contestant take a seat at the table on *The View,* unashamedly proclaiming her biblical worldview during Hot Topics. She held her own and was not afraid to go back and forth with opinionated heavyweights Barbara Walters, Whoopi Goldberg, and Joy Behar who, the majority of the time, were in total disagreement with her. I remember hearing her speak faithfully, stand firmly, yet listen with empathy—never afraid to apologize if she misunderstood or had a logical, reasonable, or compassionate change of heart. She never wavered. This woman was a powerhouse, yet she was graceful. I watched wonderstruck as she grew her voice and career before my eyes, and I cheered her on from the sidelines like millions of others.

From a distance I watched a woman just one year younger than I am carve out her path in an industry I've grown up in my whole life. She was so strong, so bold and unafraid to walk into the fire. How did she have that kind of confidence? Where did her courage and strength come from? How has she been able to hold leadership positions and climb the corporate ladder, all while proclaiming her Christian faith and holding her family so tightly that you knew they were her world? How did she develop her worldview in a way that she feels so certain of it? She's a stand-out, but not in ways the entertainment industry typically embraces.

Elisabeth is someone I've always looked up to, taking note of her life and career simply because she has walked the road less traveled and paved the way for many women, like me, to feel confident enough that it can be done. We can be strong, we can be vocally conservative, and we can rise to a position of influence while keeping our dignity, morality, and values. We can be feminine, we can be beautiful and lovely, and we can have families and make them our priority while still being in the workplace. This woman is the kind of empowered woman I admired. But what I real-ized through watching her journey was that she was empowered because she was inpowered by the Holy Spirit.

An empowered woman believes she can do anything because her own strength, courage, boldness, and drive are enough. An inpowered woman believes she can do anything because God is enough. God holds all those attributes and more and supplies them to every one of us, even when we don't think we're capable of carrying them.

I never imagined as I watched Elisabeth for so many years on televi-sion that I would one day take the very same seat she held for ten years on *The View*. Scared out of my mind to be the token conservative and not feeling equipped to handle my new job, I knew I could do it because Elisabeth had done it with the same God of the universe and with the same Holy Spirit that inpowers her as He does me. "Be strong and coura-geous. Do not be afraid; do not be discouraged, for the LORD your God will be with you wherever you go" (Joshua 1:9).

Elisabeth lives out her life exactly the way she preaches it in this book. Before my cohosting position was announced to the public, Elisabeth got my number and texted me congratulations with an offer for lunch or dinner at her home or in the city or anywhere, really, that was convenient for me. She was offering me any guidance and encouragement she could provide. That wasn't the only text during my time in New York City, as she was often prompted to let me know she was praying for me, cheering me on, and available any time I needed an ear or advice.

I looked to Elisabeth as the one who went before me, knowing I could learn from her faithfulness, as well as her hardships. Views from a distance—with a wide-angle lens—have had a great impact on me. You, my friend and reader, with this book right here in your hands, are getting the intimate, up-close-and-personal tight-angle lens to obtain her wisdom. Read it with the same intentionality you would give a newly budding and growing friendship with her, as I have, to encourage and guide you in the most important areas of life, all while being in God focus.

I wish I could have walked alongside Elisabeth starting twenty years ago, sharing giggles, secrets, and tears, because I know her example of heart, character, and integrity would have ministered to me long before I knew how much I'd need and appreciate it. Knowing her personally now makes me that much more excited for you to get to learn and glean from all the life lessons she so vulnerably and humbly shares in this book. Just like Elisabeth, my worldview came into focus when my focus shifted to Him, Jesus Christ. God changes our point of view when we understand just how blurry our vision really is without Him.

—CANDACE CAMERON BURE,
actress, author, producer

1

Learning to
See Differently

You are the God who sees me.

—GENESIS 16:13

As a fourth grader, I thought I could see perfectly. After all, I made good grades and participated in school, my cursive handwriting was on point, and all my spelling tests seemed to check out okay. Didn't all the other students walk up to the chalkboard to see the spelling words and then sharpen their pencils? Or was that just me?

The smell of the mildewed sponges used to wash the chalkboards at the end of each day is still clear in my memory. But looking back, I know that was about the only thing clear to me at the time.

When the day came for us to report to the school library for our annual vision test, I stood in line obediently, smoothing my navy-blue plaid jumper over my midsection. I kept thinking, *Next year I won't be stuck in this thing. I'll finally get to wear the fifth-grade skirt and blouse,* yet knowing I was an entire school year away from that rite of passage. I felt we waited in line *forever.* I needed to stay focused. It was almost my turn.

Finally, the school nurse called my name, and I stepped my Mary Jane shoes to the masking tape on the library floor.

"Place this plastic piece over your right eye, and tell me what you see," she said.

"Okay. And now the left," she continued.

When I wasn't thinking about my uniform, I was listening carefully to students ahead of me as they read the letters on the vision chart. I had memorized them, which is why I confidently told the nurse what they were. I had figured out over the years that the benefit of having a last name that began with *F* and not with *A* was that I never really went first for anything. Even when the teacher reversed alphabetical order to give students with last names beginning with *T* or *W* a chance to go earlier, I was still in the middle. That definitely had its advantages on vision testing day.

Once I had aced the test, the nurse said, "Okay, next student please step up."

That's how it went each year.

The nurse had no idea that I had a secret. I knew I could not see the letters, but she didn't! Saved by the power of my good memory! As long as I could repeat what I had heard, I wouldn't have to get glasses.

Or so I thought. Despite my faking success on the eye exam, one of my teachers mentioned to my parents that she thought an eye doctor should examine me. I was mortified!

"Your teacher is helping you," my parents told me.

Treason is what her recommendation felt like to me. Betrayal. *The worst.*

A week or so later, I found myself in the eye doctor's office without anyone with an *A–E* last name ahead of me in line to tell me what the letters on the chart were. There was no alphabetical order to grant me time to figure out the sequence. It was just me—and the eye doctor.

"Well," he said, "I don't know how you have been doing your schoolwork because you really need glasses. You are not seeing anything clearly."

That didn't seem true to me. I was just fine. I just had to get really, *really* close to something, and then it looked clear.

I grumbled as I grew quietly curious. *What have I been missing?* I wondered. *What more will I really be able to see if I get glasses? Will things look different? Will they look better? Worse?*

With the glasses prescription in hand, my mom and I darted to Lens-

Crafters. I can still remember the parking spot we pulled into. I knew this excursion was important. What I did not know was that I would never see the same again.

With the guarantee that my glasses could be done in less than an hour, we began our search for the perfect frames. I must have tried on every pair while my mom waited patiently and helped me. And then I was ready. The decision was made.

With a familiar, encouraging-but-protective voice, my mom asked, "Are you sure about these frames? As long as you like them, that's all that matters."

Like them? I thought. I loved them! They were the biggest, reddest, widest lenses I could ever have imagined, and in about fifty-nine minutes, they would hold the power to let me see all the things the eye doctor said I had been missing.

"Yes, Mom. These will be great." I was sure.

While the people at LensCrafters made my lenses, I ran errands with my mom, as she had taken the afternoon off from work for the big event. The sky grew darker, and the big fuzzy red lights on the backs of the cars in front of us told me it was almost dinnertime. My stomach sent the same message with its growling. I was getting hungry—and a little nervous.

Mom and I returned to the eyeglass store fifty-five minutes after we had left, and *there they were.*

Putting on those glasses for the first time was something I will never forget.

I finally saw what I had been missing out on all those years. The leaves on the trees—I could see them from across the street, and I could see *all* of them! I could see everything on the wall from all the way across the room! Those fuzzy red car lights were not fuzzy at all! Even better, they were not just one big blob of red blurry light. There were two—and they were sharp and square! (I am dating myself. These were the days before the innovative third brake light.)

I could read street signs for the very first time. I spent the entire ride home calling them out: "Papa Gino's!" "CVS pharmacy!" "Dry cleaners!" "Kmart!" "Gulf!"

I could see people—their faces and their expressions.

My mom had the biggest smile on her face—and a little tear. I had been faking her out with my way of being okay with the blur for so long that she likely felt both overjoyed that I could finally see and perplexed and guilty about not catching it earlier. It was not her fault at all. She was the smartest, most caring mom (and she still is). I was just really good at memorizing eye charts.

Seeing as Others Do

I was seeing everything for the first time. I mean, really seeing everything, not just knowing it was there. There is a huge difference. And I never ever wanted to be without that ability again. My first time wearing glasses was also when I learned that the way I saw things wasn't necessarily the way others did—nor was my blurry or clear necessarily the "right way." Those big red glasses showed me that sometimes others had a completely different view of the world around them.

Even though this lesson was in the physical sense of sight, I soon learned that the same truth applied in the metaphorical sense. The way I looked at a situation or an issue might not be the same way someone else saw it—and it would take more than a pair of glasses to make sense of this. I realized that we all have our own point of view, based on our experiences, our education, and our outlook. Merriam-Webster online defines *point of view* as "a position or perspective from which something is considered or evaluated." This distinction became very important when I began my broadcasting career.

One of the first lessons I learned about conducting interviews is that extracting the point of view, or POV, of the person being interviewed is essential. Doing so allows the interviewer the chance to see the issue or topic through the other person's eyes. Getting as close as possible to seeing the truth of the matter from that person's viewpoint is the goal. Almost always, seeing the story as that person sees it requires a shift in perspective. For decades I have practiced and refined the skill of extracting the POV of the person I am interviewing to get to the truth of the matter.

Seeing Through God's Lens

My first shift from seeing everything through fuzzy eyes to seeing with crystal clarity happened in 1985. Little did I know that, years later, I would use the recollection of this event to illustrate the love of God and His vision for all of us.

I've learned that adjusting my point of view has at least two benefits: it allows me to see things the way someone else does, and spiritually it allows me to take that to the next level and see things as God wants me to see them. My hope has been that my vision would move further away from my own thoughts, opinions, and interpretations and closer to the way God sees things.

I tell this intimate journey of faith through the important moments in my life, moments of my life's story that have caused me to see something differently than the way God wanted me to see it and the sometimes rocky but always revealing ways He has led me to see situations His way. From *Survivor* to *The View* to *FOX & Friends* to my current role as

CBO (Chief Breakfast Officer for my husband and three children)—
through being hired, fired, and retired—He has allowed me to be inspired, and I have learned a lot the hard way.

Despite my naturally strong work ethic, which has given me a tendency to will my way through situations, my constant prayer of surrender
is that by the power of the Holy Spirit, I will line up my point of view
behind the lens of the gospel in order to see myself, others, and all that is
happening as God wants me to see it. I pray to see myself as He sees me
and as He sees my situations. As you read through these pages, this is my
prayer for you too.

That ability—to see clearly through the biggest, widest lens possible—is a blessing I do not take for granted. My point of view has been
refined and changed and adjusted, but it comes into sharp, clear focus
when I look through the lens of God's promises. The lessons I have
learned—some powerful, some practical, and some intimately personal—
have all been blessings. His lens is there, and I have the blessing and
opportunity to *choose* to look through my lens alone (limited) or His
(limitless).

My lens looks like fear; His looks like trust.

My lens can look like disappointment; His looks like hope.

My lens can look deceiving; His looks like truth.

I have learned the hard way that mistaking our vision for God's
heavenly lens only allows *us* to define our days, our years, or ourselves
incorrectly—and things get out of line quickly. I now know that I don't
want to look at anything without the lens of Scripture. Believe me, I have
tried to see things on my own. Thankfully, God has brought some amazing hearts, friends, and teachers into my story to press into my heart, encourage me, and redirect me to that big pair of glasses so that I see through
His lens—time and time again. Within the pages of this book, you will

meet those who have taught me—the spiritual optometrists who have helped me look at something differently or more closely and pointed my eyes to a different point of view. Those lessons and moments are precious to me.

As I look back on this adventure-packed path that God has placed me on—from being a walk-on college-softball player from Cranston, Rhode Island, to dropping into the Australian outback by plane on season 2 of *Survivor*, to voicing my thoughts and opinions on *The View*, to hosting a news program on the FOX News Channel—I still blink a few times! This journey assures me that God has already written my story. He's been there all along, at every juncture, failure, and next turn, putting things back into focus. He is the ultimate lens crafter.

In my mind, I am still that little girl who wants to get the biggest pair of glasses possible and see things the way God sees them. I've come a long way since that day in the eye doctor's office.

I want you to feel invited and welcomed into the points of view I have witnessed, experienced, and learned from. They range from moments on the infield to dinner with Queen Elizabeth II.

My sight is not perfect. My point of view constantly needs to be refocused. You will learn throughout this book that I am a fixer-upper, a work in progress. I know that God is not done with me yet. Remember, I tend to learn the hard way! Most of that work begins with my point of view and perspective. What I've learned is that until I see myself as God sees me, I am not seeing clearly, and until I see God in everything, I am not seeing at all. I hope that in my journey you are able to recognize a little bit of yours and that you will learn, as I am learning, to see your story from God's point of view and trust that it is far ahead of all your circumstances. So let's put on those big red glasses together, figuratively speaking, and see all that He wants us to see.

2

The Walk-On Way

I know who you are, and I know what you
can do. I love you. Go show them.

—Dad

I tend to do things "the walk-on way." This means that whatever I lacked in natural talent or ability I made up for with hard work, determination, and persistence. I can characterize a lot of my life this way: working hard worked for me. Maybe I didn't have the skill to do certain things better than everyone else, but I never let that stop me.

I am more than blessed to have been raised in a home where faith, freedom, and family were the pillars of my youth. My mom and dad raised me to understand that believing in God, working hard, and having gratitude held doors open. If a door was open, I was going to work hard to go through it and to help others through it as well.

My parents—both of them—had an amazing work ethic. Our house rules went like this: Work hard. Be kind. Be honest.

My dad and mom told me that if I worked hard, I could do whatever I wanted to in life. What they failed to mention was that no matter how hard I worked at shooting hoops outside until dinnertime, it was not likely that I could play in the WNBA (I am all of five foot five). Yet they allowed me to play in the possible and not just the probable.

Nonetheless, I would not go inside until I reached my goal of a certain number of shots in a row on the street under the lights. If I made just one more shot, I would be one shot closer to my goal.

At some point on my journey, I allowed a little lie to become a big part of my life. It said, "You might not *be* the best, but you can try to *work harder* than the rest." I came to believe that the more I efforted through something, the more valuable I was. I became convinced that the harder I worked, the better I was. Struggle and hard work should look like a big sacrifice and hurt a lot, I thought, and I found myself craving hard work—in everything I did. What I did not realize is that freedom can come with an understanding that resting well is key to working well.

Called by Name

I played softball for years growing up, and my dad was always there for my games. He was my coach for almost all my softball playing days, and he never missed a practice. When I played he coached me from the side-lines, and after every game he talked to me about how I played and what to do differently so I could improve.

Mostly though, my dad saw who I was, not just what I did. Where I saw mistakes, he saw capabilities and adjustments. That's because he didn't see only a passed ball or a strikeout, or even a solid base hit. He saw me.

The work ethic my parents instilled in me, coupled with my dad's coaching, encouragement, and belief in me, paid off when the time came for me to go to Boston College. What a hard season that was! My mom was battling breast cancer, and I had a heavy heart going into what was the biggest change during the most uncertain time my family had ever known.

When I confessed to my mom that I did not want to go and leave her during her treatment, she said to me, "Go. You must go. I'll be fine."

Art and sports had always been my outlet, and my mom and dad let me grow in both. As the time to depart for school drew near, I knew I would have a work-study job at the museum, would double major in biology and studio art, and would be in the premedical program, but something was missing from those plans, and my dad knew it.

"Why don't you try out for the softball team?" he asked casually as we were loading up the car.

I thought he was joking.

"Dad," I said, "they are Division I. They're in the Big East Conference." (At that time they were.) I continued, "I'll never make the team. They have all their scholarship players already. They don't even know me. I'm not good enough."

I battled fear, followed by doubt, followed by the lie: *They don't even know your name.*

Partially to honor my dad and partially because I had a little hope placed in me that day, I packed my glove and my bat bag.

After arriving at school, I got my dorm room organized with the best roommate in the whole wide world, Jennie. God sure blessed me with her friendship then and now. Then I reached out to the softball coach and found out what day tryouts would be held. And I called my dad to let him know that I was going for it. He could tell I was terrified.

My dad simply said, "I know who you are, and I know what you can do. I love you. Go show them." He was serious and I knew it.

Then he added, "You can run really fast. Go do that."

So I did.

I pressed on through the next day of tryouts. Ground balls spitting up in my face, sprints, push-ups—and the fact that I must have missed every ball hit to me. Every single one.

Ooh, was I angry. Almost in tears, I called my dad and explained how awful the tryout was.

"Give it another try," he told me. "Show up tomorrow, and give it another try."

Fine. I would do that, but that was it.

The next morning, I literally fell out of my dorm-room bed because I was so sore. But in a way, knowing I was far from my mom, who was in the battle of her life against cancer, put things in perspective and gave the pain and fear I had inside a place where it made sense on the outside. As tired as I was, and as hurt as I was, getting it all out on the field felt healthy. That had been my way, and I would give it another try.

On day two of tryouts, I ran even harder, helped with equipment, and decided to bunt—a lot—not because I was great at bunting, but because with a bunt, at least my bat had a better chance of hitting the ball. I kept thinking, *The bigger I swing, the bigger I will miss.*

I've learned since then that the truth is, you don't miss bigger if you swing bigger. If you miss, you miss—no matter how hard you swing.

When the tryouts were complete, I could hardly wait for the coaches to finish calling the names of the players who made the team. As I heard them read one name after another, my heartbeat was intense. I could hardly wait for them to finish so I could put the softball team behind me and move forward with my college experience. Just before they did, I heard the last name called.

"Filarski," they said.

What?

I made the team!

They called my name.

It didn't matter that it was the last name on the list. It mattered that they called my name. I would get a number and a helmet and a jersey and my name on the roster.

That first year and the following year, I was the happiest benchwarmer on the planet! I was so happy to simply be a part of it all. Cheers from the bench? I was on it. Carrying water jugs? You bet. Organizing equipment in the dugout? I had that covered. Warming up the starting outfielders? Sure! I was so thrilled to be on the team that whatever I could do to help, I did.

I do have a confession: during warm-ups, I tried to dive for every ball if I thought it would result in a grass stain or a streak of mud on my uniform—just to look like I had played in the game.

A time came when bench warming became pinch running, meaning that when one of the players could not run the bases, I ran for her. That was my role, and I was happy with it. And whenever I did have a chance to hit the ball, I swung fully, freely, and joyfully.

God's Top Recruit

Maybe you can relate, and you're thinking, *I know what she means!* Maybe you too have worked *so hard* all your life as well.

Working like a walk-on—whether you're on a sports team, at home with your family, at work, in relationships with friends, or another setting—is not a bad thing. It is about the *why* behind the *work*. In fact, I really like Colossians 3:23, which says: "Whatever you do, work at it with all your heart, as working for the Lord, not for human masters." But the freedom of working hard at whatever you do comes from knowing that God does not see you as a walk-on. God sees you as His top recruit.

Just as my dad always saw me for who I was, God sees you for who you are. He knows your name. He has a jersey and a locker and a cap with your name on it. He has saved a place for you and has paid your way through life in full. Let me explain this by asking you to imagine a scenario.

Let's say you get a letter in the mail tomorrow. When you read it, you can hardly believe what it says. It comes from someone you don't know, and it promises that if you have kids, each of your children has already been accepted at his or her first-choice college or university. All of them. Even your five-year-old. They are all accepted—exactly as they are right now. The school is holding places for them. Their spots are secure, just waiting for them to come. The whole college acceptance thing? It's a done deal. Each child is accepted. You are fully accepted.

In addition, all tuition and all the fees are paid—completely. Every single dime. Everyone has a full scholarship. Why? Because each one is a top recruit.

Your first comments would probably be "Who would do this for us? Who paid for all of this? I want to meet that person and thank him!" Of course you would.

Imagine the extraordinary kindness of a person who could and would guarantee that all your children could attend the schools of their choosing at no cost whatsoever. Imagine a person who would do this simply because he wanted to take the college decision drama and the cost burden off your shoulders. Just think about it. What if that really happened one day?

That scenario is a tiny example of what God has already done for us. It represents His love and care for us. He loved us before we deserved His love (because we didn't) and before we earned it (because we couldn't). We are fully accepted. That acceptance has been paid for in full—on the cross with Christ's blood. Imagine *that*.

Metaphorically speaking, the scholarship has been saved for you. All the fees have been paid in advance—in the best place you could ever imagine being. I want to encourage you right now to rest in the truth that you have already been recruited as God's first choice. You are on full scholarship to heaven. It's the only place where good looks or brains or athletic abilities or awards from your job won't help you earn a spot. Your place has already been reserved for you. It's paid for.

That raises the same question as the scholarships to your children's first-choice colleges would raise: Who would do this for me? And just as you would want to meet and thank a person who would extend such generosity and relieve such a burden from your family, you would want to meet, know, and thank the One who has secured your spot in heaven:

Who did this for me? Who is the Jesus who did this for people?

"I am the God of heaven and earth, who gave My only Son for you. The debt is paid because I want to be with you again."

Seeing ourselves as God's top recruits points not only to *who* we are but also to *whose* we are. So let's look at the team! Our awesome God loves you enough to pay the deposit in full for you to have a secured spot in heaven. This spot does not require that you work hard to earn it, as you would not be able to do that. You can be free to swing away. You will miss sometimes, but this heavenly Father recruits you by name, knows your number, wants to be with you, and has saved you a spot. The price—that tuition fee—has been paid in full by His Son, Jesus Christ, our Savior, who took our place and came to earth to pay the price for us to live forever.

I know this is a simplified example. But I am not ever going to fully understand what God has done, because it flows from such radical love and desire for an imperfect me. In this example, though, I see how I can live as though I am recruited and called by name, or I can keep trying to earn God's love and a place in heaven by my own works. But the reality is, I can never earn that spot because it has already been purchased for me.

Father Knows Best

I still think about what my dad said to me as he took me to college in 1995. Years after he spoke those words, it dawned on me that what he said reflects what our heavenly Father is saying to us all the time: "I know who you are, and I know what you can do. I love you. Go show them."

Just as my dad knew me and wanted me to play softball the way he knew I was made to play, with all the joy that went into it, God knows us and wants us to do what He created us to do. He sees us and hears our hearts. He wants us to hear His voice telling us that He knows who we are—everything about us—and has made us to fulfill the great purpose and plan He has in mind for us. We don't have to hope to make the team because He has already called us by name and we are His. Isaiah 43:1 summarizes this perfectly: "But now, thus says the LORD, who created you, O Jacob, and He who formed you, O Israel: 'Fear not, for I have redeemed you; I have called you by your name; You are Mine'" (NKJV).

When I think about God having called us by name and reserved a place for us, I think of the National Football League draft. Other people may not think of that, but I'm a player's wife. I have spent a *lot* of time around the NFL. When draft picks are announced, it's a big deal. In a televised event, each player's name is called, and he receives a jersey with his name on it and a hat. Immediately. Once he's chosen, he's part of the team.

God is excited to have you belong to Him too. In fact, He can hardly wait for you to accept the spot He has reserved for you. He knows you did not earn the spot; that was not an option. It's a gift. He is not asking you to change or become better; He wants you just the way you are. He knows you really don't deserve it, and He knows He will never trade you for anything or anyone. Ever. Because *you are His*.

As you go about your life, pursuing His purpose for you, God wants you to swing like you are already on the team, not like you are simply trying out. There are a couple of Scripture verses that are important to me when I think about this. One is Zechariah 4:6, in which God says, "Not by might nor by power, but by my Spirit." This verse has always encouraged me to rest and find freedom in the fact that doing what God wants me to do is not up to me alone. I don't have to do it by myself. His Spirit is my helper (John 14:26), and He is yours too. The other verse is Philippians 4:13: "I can do all this through him who gives me strength." Both verses make essentially the same point—that when you and I belong to God, we can count on Him to help us and strengthen us to do everything He wants us to do. We can take the swing; He's in charge of connecting it with the ball.

You can rest in the fact that you are chosen. You are God's top recruit. So put on your jersey knowing you have made the team. All you have to do now is show up and get into the game!

3

Who Packs Your Chute?

Your love, LORD, reaches to the heavens,
your faithfulness to the skies.

—PSALM 36:5

Once I finished college, I could see the future unfolding ahead of me. Still living in Boston, I had a job as a shoe designer for Puma that paid well and allowed me to be creative—the perfect outlet for my passion for art and sports—and I enjoyed it thoroughly. Relationally, life could not have been better. I was in love. Tim and I had been dating for three years. His family had even opened their home and hearts to me. They even invited me to live with them during the previous year so I could save money to get my own place with a roommate. During my senior year in college, I ran—and finished—the Boston Marathon. My mom, in the marathon for her life, had won her battle with breast cancer and reached the five-year clear mark.

Getting used to drinking coffee, the grind of real life, and paying off student loans was enough. It was obvious that through my hard work, the kindness of others, and amazing opportunities, God had provided all I could ask for and more. Yet I did love setting a goal, and there was something in me that yearned for the next challenge.

One day, one of my fellow shoe designers mentioned applying for "a game that challenges you by throwing you in the middle of nowhere to see what you're made of and if you would survive." That struck a curious nerve in me and, oddly, sounded enticing.

What am I made of? I wondered.

I knew I could find out or at least get some significant answers by being in the middle of nowhere by myself, without any of the people who had always caught me when I fell in the past, without those who picked me up, brushed me off, and set me back on my journey with their love and encouragement.

As I investigated the "game," which was actually a television show that would take place in Australia, I learned it would involve hunger, adventure, friends, enemies, climbing, falling, long days, long nights, wallabies, crocodiles, and breathtaking sunsets—all in a country that serves as a habitat for nine of the world's ten deadliest snakes. Yes, if I did that, I would learn a lot about what I was made of and what makes me tick. Looking back now, I can say that I learned much more about my maker than about what I was made of.

Under intense deadline pressure, I decided to complete the application, which I submitted on pieces of paper grocery bags bound with twine (very rustic-looking, I thought, and sure to stand out from other applications). In addition, I had to submit a videotape of myself explaining why I should be the next Survivor. In exchange for pizza, my roommate's brother filmed it for me as I drove through the streets of Boston making my case. It even includes the part when my beat-up white Volkswagen Jetta slammed into a massive pothole. Because of the deadline, we had no time to re-shoot the video, so I sent it, pothole jolt and all. After the adrenaline rush of applying for the show subsided, I waited.

A letter and a phone call followed, indicating that I had made the next round of interviews. To calm my nerves and jitters, I decided to run to the interview instead of driving or taking public transportation. I ran for a full hour.

I arrived just in time, sweating like crazy, and answered a series of questions, then answered more questions, and then had my picture taken. They asked if I was sweating because of nerves.

"No," I said, "I ran here."

"Did you not have a ride?" they asked.

"No, I just like to run."

"How will you get back?" they wanted to know.

"I'll run."

That was their last question—and my last answer—of the day.

The running and the sweating turned out to be okay with them, I guess, because some time later they let me know that I was among the final contestants, and they asked me to spend a week in Los Angeles. Before leaving Boston, I worked extra hours so I could take off for what was turning out to be an adventure!

I made the most of my first trip to the West Coast and quickly discovered that my favorite part of each day was a morning run in Santa Monica. My least favorite parts were sitting in the hotel room having to be ready for unannounced interviews and unplanned meals. The producers only allowed us one hour of free time outside each day. I passed the hours praying, reading, doodling, and calling home.

One day, I noticed how many scarves I had brought from Boston; each one reminded me of someone or something. So much time in a hotel room had gotten to me, so I created a headdress out of the scarves and wore it the next time someone called me for an interview.

The producers paused awkwardly and looked at me when they saw it.

I explained to them that I planned to take it as my "survival item" and wear it wherever they sent us for the show to remind me of who I am and what is important to me. It would be my "immunity" headdress.

Before I left that interview, someone asked me what I would think about being on an island with a really good-looking guy. There was no possibility at all that I would be interested in that because Tim had my heart. If that was what they wanted, then what I wanted was for them to

stop wasting my time and send me home. After I grabbed a handful of
M&M'S and ate them, still wearing my headdress, I heard the producers
say, "Thank you. You can go now."

That, for sure, was the end of the road. And I was frustrated—really
frustrated. I had wasted the week thinking this show was the way to test
myself for sure. But if all they wanted was some tropical dating game, I
was beyond disappointed. But I knew that it was better to let them know
the truth than to give them *any* room to think there was *any* possibility
of that.

Back in my hotel room, packing to return to Boston, I heard a knock
on the door. Mark Burnett and a couple of producers announced, "You
made it! Now pack your things. You're booked on the first plane to Texas,
where you'll attend jump school. Once you get through the certification
there, you'll be on *Survivor*!"

I made it? I could hardly believe it (especially after the headdress incident). After a bit more conversation, I learned that all I had to do now
was extend my time off from work for a few days, go to Texas, and jump
out of a plane—*ten* times.

The team continued, "Here's cash to find yourself a place to stay and
for your lessons. There's a motel in Giddings, Texas. You'll have to find
the jump school and get yourself there."

For privacy reasons, they added, I would travel under the name
Amanda.

"That sounds like a plan," I said to myself. In my opinion, it sounded
like a *bad* plan but a plan nonetheless. I was in. After all, I had come so
far at that point. I needed and wanted to move forward.

I took the envelope containing cash, an airline ticket, and a piece of
paper that included some—but not much—information about my activi-
ties over the next several days and finished packing my belongings.

On My Own

I don't remember much about the next morning or the flight, as it was likely early and uneventful. Once I landed in Austin, Texas, I found a taxi and gave the address to the driver, trying to sound certain about where I was going.

"That will be a two-hour drive, ma'am," he said.

"Yes, I know. Thanks." It sounded convincing, despite my anxiety.

After traveling lots of open roads and highway and ending up on a dirt farm road that seemed to reach to the end of the earth, we finally came to a motel with a blinking sign and trucks pulled up to it. As I looked at the row of metal doors, I told myself, "This is it."

My instincts kicked in, and I began to feel a little apprehensive. The taxi driver looked in the rearview mirror, and though he didn't say anything, I am sure he wondered what I was doing there.

Inside my motel room, the first action I took was to push the tattered vinyl chair from the desk in front of the door. I think the last time I did that was as a teenager playing a trick on a friend during a game of hide-and-seek. This time it was not a game. It seemed necessary. After a long day of travel and wanting to go for a run (my trusted stress-relief method), yet not feeling comfortable enough with my surroundings to do so, I settled for doing push-ups and squats and jumping rope in my room.

I made a phone call to the jump school listed on the paper Mark had given me. I was told they were expecting me, and the call ended with, "We'll see you tomorrow, Amanda."

Still unaccustomed to the fake name, I paused and said slowly, "Yes, see you then."

After that, a harsh reality set in: The motel was not close to the jump school, and I was low on cash. After looking through the phone book in the room, I tried to find a nearby rental car place but was unsuccessful. The next best thing was a car dealership, so I determined to set out on foot to find it the next morning.

In a moment of reflection, I thought, *My mom would kill me if she knew I was going to jump out of a plane tomorrow.* I decided against telling her. She would want to see the paperwork and insurance, and she'd want assurance that I would be safely returned home. She would worry. But I was on a mission. I would get to go on the adventure of a lifetime if I could get through that week. I had to do it.

Adrenaline had kept me going for most of the day, but I now realized I was hungry. I walked to the front desk and asked, "Where's the closest place to get something to eat?"

"Closest," the front desk attendee replied, "and about the *only* place to eat is the smothered ribs joint down the road." He pointed in the direction of a cabin with some lights on. I had no choice. It was the ribs joint or nothing.

The restaurant was a family business, and while I was there, I was the only person who was not a family member. Before I could decide if that was good or bad, the family gathered around me and asked my name. Conflicted as I was, not good at lying, yet under strict instructions to not tell anyone my real name or why I was there, I cringed and said, "Amanda."

"You sure?" the female asked. I must have sounded as unsure as I felt.

I responded with a weak, uncertain smile.

"What brings you here? To Giddings?" someone asked.

"Well, I'm just traveling some," I said. That was true. It just wasn't full disclosure.

"What do you do for work?" a young boy asked.

"I draw." Also true. My job as a shoe designer involved lots of drawing. It was a good thing I went with that because the next question would put my "occupation" to the test.

"Can you draw me?" the little guy asked.

"I sure can."

As I began to sketch, I concluded that my gig with the alias was not so bad after all. It seemed to be working.

I finished drawing about the time my food arrived. After I thanked the family, left money for the meal and a tip, I headed back to the motel, leaving the sketch behind.

The walk back was dark and lonely. Relieved to be standing in front of my room, I could barely get the key into the lock. "Please, God, protect me," I prayed. "Just please keep me safe."

Back in my room I thought, *Tomorrow is a big day. I need to get a car and jump out of a plane ten times. No big deal, right?* Somehow I managed to wrestle fear to the mat and go to sleep.

Ready to Jump!

The alarm buzzed loudly the next morning, but not as loud as the gears of the tractor trailer cranking just beyond my window. Cautiously, after some push-ups and a breakfast bar and water, I waited for the coast to clear outside my room. For whatever reason, the fake identity made me feel like I was a criminal or something!

With the car dealership's address in hand, I walked for what felt like hours down a dusty highway until I finally got there.

A man, presumably the salesman, approached me. "Can I help you, miss?" he asked.

"Do you have cars to rent?"

"We sell cars here, ma'am. Sorry."

The words tumbled out of my mouth. "I need to get to jump school today. I have no way to get there, and the school is more than an hour away. And I have to be there! They're expecting me."

I finished by saying, "I don't have enough money to buy a car."

He said, "The only car not for sale here is mine."

He then apologized once more and left me standing in the midst of his inventory feeling defeated.

"Sir!" I shouted. "This is really important. I have a hundred dollars. Can I rent your car for a hundred dollars? I'll bring it back each day for the next two days until I complete my training. Please. Can I rent your car?"

For some reason, he said yes. After unlocking a child's car seat from the back and removing it, he handed me the key.

"Okay, you can rent it each day until you're finished," he said. "Just drive safe. I need it back in good form. One hundred dollars."

"Yes. A hundred dollars. I have that. Thank you for doing this."

Car? Check.

Next on the list: jump out of a plane.

Off I went, with an old cell phone and a map, down another long dusty road. Finally, in the distance I saw a small building and some type of little kite or flag flying.

That's got to be the jump school, I assured myself.

As the car approached the small building, I wondered once more why on earth that man let me use *his* car.

I could hardly believe I was finally there—at the jump school. Three men greeted me, and one said, "You must be Amanda."

Gulp. "Yes."

He continued, "We're excited to get you ready for your honeymoon."

Honeymoon? What *honeymoon?*

"Your fiancé wants to parachute you into your honeymoon. Now *that* is cool," another man said.

"I'm just a little nervous," I said with a smile, trying to get my mind caught up on the fake details of my life.

"Well, you should be," one man joked.

"Don't listen to a word he says, but be nice to him," another chimed in. "He packs the chutes."

Here We Go

"Now, let's get you some ground training," someone said. That sounded better than anything we might do in the air. I realized I was more apprehensive than I thought—and that I was totally alone.

The training involved a simulator of sorts. I was wearing an altitude-measuring device on my chest. The instructor taught me what to say at different elevation levels and when to look down at the measuring device. The whole teaching session felt like a dream, almost unreal, because I did not really want to jump. But I knew I had to. I paid attention, studied, and listened closely.

They kept repeating a phrase I didn't understand at first. "Eat the carrot," they said. It seemed important to them, but all it did for me was make me hungry. They finally explained that *Eat the carrot* meant I should look for the tapered orange flag waving from a stick on the ground and aim for its point, because that would indicate I was landing with the wind in the chute. *Eat the carrot* meant keeping my chute inflated with the wind in my face so that as I approached the ground, the wind would act as a brake and slow me down enough to hit the ground running at a speed I could handle.

There is a big difference between learning not to fall and learning to soar. Unfortunately for me, I seemed to be learning instead to fall and not to soar.

After ground training and a snack that consisted of water, some peanut butter in a jar, and half of a protein bar, one of the men said, "Now let's get you a jumpsuit!"

That sounded terrible to me. But not as terrible as falling from the sky.

What am I about to do? And ten *times?!*

Altitude, wingman, eat the carrot. Those words ran through my head robotically.

I wanted to run to the car and drive as fast as possible away from the jump school, but before I could do that, I was dressed in a fluorescent pink jumpsuit and holding a pair of goggles.

I walked around the back of the school, saw the guy packing bags, and gulped. *Those are the chutes,* I told myself as I remembered a previous instruction. *Smile at that guy. He packs the chutes.*

The chute packer caught my eye and gave me an odd grin. Likely because I was staring. Likely because I was making him as nervous as I felt.

My stomach turned.

That is whose hands I am putting my life in? I asked myself.

I don't even know you! I screamed inside my head.

There was no time to protest, get to know him, or ask any more questions.

"You ready?" someone asked.

Before I could come up with a reason not to be ready, we loaded up in the small plane. The engine roared, and the ground soon looked farther and farther away. The jump school slipped out of sight, and the door of the plane seemed like the mouth of a lion to me. The turmoil I felt inside and the adrenaline running through me left my fingers numb. Inside I was screaming, yet the instructor and pilot had a demeanor of quiet calm. The rush of air matched the rush of fear. *I got myself into this. But God would have to get me out . . . and down safely.*

It was time.

There I was, with a jumper on each side of me as I clung to the bar in my hot-pink suit. I asked, "Isn't there supposed to be someone attached to me?"

"No, ma'am. To get certified, you jump ten times alone. Weather depending, we should get you halfway there today."

I am going to do this five times, I thought. And that would only be half of the task.

Check one. I moved my chest to the bar and pretended to release.

Suddenly the calm voices became loud voices, but the fear was louder, and I did not respond to their call.

Check two (the one before the real launch). *At five thousand feet, deploy your chute,* I reminded myself. *Eat the carrot.*

And . . . check.

Forfeiting my grip on the bar by the door of the plane, I tumbled and spun into the thin air at proper altitude.

At least I thought I was in thin air.

Spinning, I hit a hard surface. I opened my eyes and saw I was still inside the tiny plane. *What?*

"Amanda! Amanda! We've been calling you back into the plane. Couldn't you hear us?"

I heard them, all right. I just didn't know who they were talking to!

One of them continued, "We are not authorized to have you jump today."

What? I thought I had jumped. I know I released the bar, so they must have been pulling me back inside the plane.

I exhaled and decided I had had enough. "My name isn't Amanda!"
I told them. "It's Elisabeth!"

This resulted in three very confused men as the plane landed.

Back on the ground, someone said, "We need to get this sorted out.
Your fiancé called and doesn't want you to jump after all. He put a hold
on the paperwork . . . Wait, your name is not Amanda?"

Compared to the idea of tossing myself out of a plane ten times, this
whole massive storytelling thing seemed secondary.

After several phone calls between the jump school and someone as-
sociated with *Survivor,* who was pretending to be a wedding planner, finally someone put me on the line to talk to a producer.

"Elisabeth, tell them you have to go, that your fiancé does not want
you to jump, and that you will figure it out tonight. You need to get on a
plane tomorrow and head back to Boston."

As I hung up the phone, thinking about having to explain what was
said, my thoughts were going in a million directions. I was not able to
bear one more lie, so I told the guys from the jump school, "I think we
need to figure out if this is what we want to do."

"Jumping or getting married?" one guy joked.

At that point, nothing seemed funny.

After thanking the guys, I took the car back to its owner and thanked
that man as he reinstalled the car seat.

"Will you be back tomorrow?" he asked.

"No, sir. I finished."

"Did you make it?" he wondered.

"Oh, I made it," I said, adding silently, *out alive.*

The long walk back to the motel needed to be quick. I had to get back
before dark, and I did.

Hitting the pillow hard in anticipation of an early flight, I had to wonder if the whole experience had been a test of my will.

Back to Boston and Beyond

I woke the next morning thinking that the trip back to Boston would be dreamy—because I knew I would not have to jump out of the plane. Questions swirled in my head as I packed to go home. I had made it to the final round of *Survivor* and learned a *lot* already.

One lesson I learned is that trying to live as anyone but yourself is confusing and annoying, and it can cost you your life as the person you were meant to be. Another one is that your life is in the hands of the guy who packed the chutes.

My point of view during that season of my life was to get from point A to point B. Knowing Mark Burnett as I know him, I am now sure he had eyes on the entire situation (at least I pray he did).

One question I still ask myself is, Knowing what I know now, would I ever redo that moment?

I am not sure. It was all a means to an end. After all, the *Survivor* teams had told me, "All you have to do is get jump certified, and you are going to the outback."

I have spent years thinking deeply about the lessons I learned during that trip to Texas. Truly, they changed my perspective on a couple of key issues.

As I mentioned, I learned how important it is to be *who you are,* not someone else. God created each of us to be unique. Living as someone else will always lead to failure because it is not living as the individuals we were designed to be. I did not respond to a frantic emergency call to get back in the plane because I did not hear the men calling my name, and I was not made to respond to someone else's name.

At times, we might be able to get by, pretending to be someone we're not, but when it comes to high-altitude, high-pressure situations, we will not respond properly—and we may not respond at all—if we are not being ourselves. I remember screaming with exasperation, yet feeling so free, "My name is not Amanda! It is Elisabeth!"

All of us want to be called by name. We desire to be fully known. Why? Because that is how God designed us. He says in His Word, "Bring my sons from afar and my daughters from the ends of the earth—everyone who is called by my name, whom I created for my glory, whom I formed and made" (Isaiah 43:6–7).

I can say after this experience, if there is an area of your life in which you are trying to pretend to be or live like someone or something you are not—unless you have some sort of safety-related reason to hide—there may be some dangerous consequences. You would find the most amazing freedom in dropping the alias, the pretending, and the image you may be trying to project. The right time to be true to yourself is . . . well, always. God rescues us by calling us by name. It's hard to hear the call when you are trying to be anything but the person He is calling you to be.

When it comes to realizing that the person who packs your chute is important, I want to say that we all have some free-fall moments in life. There are risky moves and challenges involved whenever we decide to do something new or to move forward. We need to ask ourselves who is packing our chutes. In other words, who is supporting us? Are they people we would trust to catch us if not everything goes as planned?

Ultimately, I think we need to depend on God's Word to get us through every situation we face, as much as a person jumping out of a plane would depend on a functional parachute. We need people around us who know that Word, pray according to that Word, and speak that Word to us and over us. Those are the people we can trust. It's important to ask ourselves, "Who's packing my chute? Who have I trusted to get in my heart and lift me up when the wind is at my face?"

That day in Texas was not the last time I had to take a jump—literal or figurative—in life. That almost-jump happened before I even stepped foot in the Australian outback. Yet, whether the intended purpose of that parachuting excursion was to test my willingness to move forward or to refine my character for the road ahead, it was one of the most valuable experiences of my life. Since then, it has served to sharpen my point of view on staying true to whose I am and being intentional when it comes to who is packing my chute.

That day in the midst of Texas, though I did not have to make the jump, I was about to need a parachute, figuratively speaking, for all that I was going to be jumping into for the next ten years and beyond.

4

Surviving *Survivor*

❧

I will lead the blind by ways they have not known,
    along unfamiliar paths I will guide them;
I will turn the darkness into light before them
    and make the rough places smooth.
These are the things I will do;
    I will not forsake them.

—Isaiah 42:16

I did not know how to fish, camp, hunt, or sleep in the wild—or how to survive in the Australian outback. I was sporty but not huntswoman sporty. Preparing to appear on the second season of *Survivor,* which premiered January 28, 2001, I bought my first pair of cargo pants. Packing for the conditions ahead was restricted to two pairs of socks, a pair of boots, a pair of sneakers, one sport top, one bathing suit, one pair of pants, one pair of shorts, and one "survival" item. The very impractical but quite meaningful headdress that got me through the interview process was my pick for the survival item. My reason for choosing the headdress was that when I was under stress in competition, brought to the end of my physical capacity and comfort, I did not want to lose my focus on who I was and where I came from. I had depended on the visual of the headdress (though hideous) in the interview process up to this point, and I would rely on the reminders it offered me in the toughest of times ahead.

The pink scarf included in the headdress was for my mom, to honor her strength and fortitude through her battle and victory when she fought breast cancer. *Survivor* would be nothing compared to what I saw her face down and walk through. The toughest of days in the Australian outback did not come with the threat of taking my health, my body, or my life, as her great challenge did. What she bravely and gracefully gritted through and battled made her the *real* survivor; what I was doing on the reality show was a game. My mom's warrior path to becoming a breast

cancer survivor forever set the bar for me when it came to facing challenges with courage, strength, and faith. Whatever physical demands or
attacks were ahead for the finite period of time my challenge would last,
fortitude and victory had been branded on my heart because of my mom.

Before appearing on *Survivor,* I had promised myself before God not
to be anything other than who I was, no matter the circumstances. I can
remember telling the producers that I believed a person could win this
game without being mean, cutting, and hurtful. I remember some of
them looking at me, wondering if I would be right. I began the game and
went through it with that commitment as my strategy. I set my heart to
be honest and kind, trusting that would be my portion.

Packed and ready to go, I said my goodbyes to Tim and his family
and to mine. I would miss our family's Thanksgiving dinner for the first
time in my life. In an Italian home, this was a big deal. Mama lived to feed
our family and gather us all at her table. My absence would not be easy on
anyone, particularly me, who would be as far from turkey and stuffing as
I had ever been. My mom tried to pass off her worry with a smile. I knew
that look. She was terrified. But I was not. Not yet anyway.

I flew under the same alias I had used in Texas in order to keep the
happenings of the show covert. The first leg of my trip took me to the
West Coast, where a group assembled at Los Angeles International Airport, including some familiar faces I recalled seeing in the hotel elevators
during the last round of interviews. Soon we began our long flight to
Australia.

Strategic thinking led everyone to stuff themselves with airport food,
just in case.

I brought along a couple of books to prepare me, and I planned to
read until the very last minute. The first was on survival skills and would
provide me with all I needed to know, I thought, about the land of the

Australian outback. In that book, I studied the agriculture, the plants and fruits, and the animals I might encounter. I already knew that nine out of the world's ten deadliest snakes were in the outback, but I learned they were exactly where we would be "surviving," and for a moment I wanted to call the whole thing off. That book I read out of sheer desperation, cramming—purely cramming—as much information about berries, animals, and climate as I could before we landed.

One potentially lifesaving lesson I learned was that for every green leafy plant that could be eaten to keep us alive and fed, there happened to be one almost exactly identical to it that would attack the stomach's lining and lead to a painful death. I quickly decided I would rather go hungry than find out the distinction the hard way.

My second book was more strategic since it was obvious to me that I could not become an expert fisher, hiker, hunter, or camper in the outback from reading a book on a plane. Knowing a little about a lot of things might not be the best gift to a group of teammates who would surely come in as masters in some, if not all, of those areas. My strategy was to master one small task through the pages of the second book.

The second book, believe it or not, was about tying knots. It should have been about "nots," but I thought I would learn the most effective and efficient ways of tying knots so we would not waste our rope when building shelter or fishing rods. I took a risk on that, I admit, and made an educated guess that no one else would be good at knots. Plus, it was one skill I would be able to practice on my own with my shoelaces all the way to our drop in the outback.

The idea of the *Survivor* game was for sixteen contestants to be divided into teams. At one point, the teams would merge, and it would be everyone for themselves until a final survivor outlasted the rest. During the flight, I glanced up from the pages once in a while and began sizing up the crowd of contestants. The goal at hand was close observation without being creepy because, at that point, any of them could be my teammates—or my competition. I needed to know their personalities before we got there to identify their strengths and perhaps their weaknesses. That knowledge would also help me recognize any changes or differences when it came to breaking points.

As I surveyed my fellow contestants, I saw that one of them was stretching, one was doing squats, one slept, another read, some giggled, and one was fidgeting with his boots. I used these visual assessments as a baseline. They were all I had so far. What we learn by observation, I found out, is only a slice of what we learn from participation. The personalities of the fifteen *Survivor* contestants would become crystal clear in a matter of hours. Though we were all in the same boat, my instincts intimated that we might not all paddle the same way.

Let the Games Begin

After a long flight, we began our trip at a cabin that belonged to a woman named Mary in Queensland, Australia. Imagine it as a ranch house with a massive covered dining area and lots of Aussie home cooking. Mary was one of the most welcoming and hospitable women I have ever met, and she could cook. Everything tasted good, except the Vegemite. I had packed a ton of protein bars and peanut butter, as I was quietly in the midst of figuring out what had been causing me stomach pain for the past three years. I did not want the team to know, as I feared it would preclude my being selected, so even during the physical exams, I never mentioned it. At this point I did not care what hurt my tummy; I was going to stuff myself like a Thanksgiving turkey. As we were getting settled at the ranch, the glances and smiles began to feel familiar.

The producers told us to be ready "just in case" at any point. Something told me that "at any point" was about to happen. That night, I slept in my cargo boots, pants, and contact lenses. Sure enough, a loud call in the early hours of the morning announced that we were to jump out of bed and eat as much as we could in five minutes before loading up.

We drove to a site where a DHC-4 Royal Australian Air Force military aircraft, known to be able to handle the roughest terrain and for its short takeoff and landing capabilities, waited to provide our transportation from the comforts of the cabin in Queensland to the Australian outback. That plane ride tossed my stomach, and as we sat on cargo belts and looped and flipped and twisted and turned, I remember praying to God to make it all stop, to get me off the plane, and to get me home!

Eventually the hellish ride concluded, and our cargo plane hovered loudly over the dusty ground of the outback. The scene was visually confusing, but we jumped off anyway and then received our tribal assignments. Immediately, I checked my pack and huddled up with my Kucha tribe, marked by matching colored bandannas. I didn't know my teammates well at the time, but we were soon to be bonded by the most trying conditions any of us had likely faced.

Waiting for each team were a ration of supplies in a large wooden crate and a map to our campsite. I remember grabbing the lid of the crate and carrying it on top of my head for the majority of that hike, in case it would be helpful for fire or shelter. For all I had been given in emotional sense and intelligence, I lacked a sense of natural navigational direction. Though a technical disadvantage, this saved me from taking on a role that included pointing and being the boss. Instead of pointing directions and north-south instructions, both of my hands were on duty balancing the splintering set of pinewood boards above my head. At that point, I wanted to be a soldier, not a general.

Eventually, we found our way and began making our shelter. From the survival handbook I had read, I knew that shelter, water, and fire would be crucial. Without shelter, all our supplies would be ruined. Temperatures were extreme in the outback, and shelter would provide us cover from both the blistering sun and the heat of the day and the cold that came at night. In addition, if done right, the shelter would protect us from the wicked rain that would accompany the onset of the wet season we could expect during our time there.

We had the rope we had saved from our supplies being tied together, and I was vocal about being able to tie knots well, without creating waste, and about suggesting the best knots for each situation. With that, I was given the job of being the person in charge of knots. I learned that having one skill to bring to the table was enough to be of value for the time being. My work ethic came in handy as we tirelessly gathered supplies and tied and built until we had a place to call home. Our lean-to shelter ultimately became home to us, at least for the near future, and from it we would have to operate like family. A scripture stayed on my mind: "Since you are my rock and my fortress, for the sake of your name lead and guide me" (Psalm 31:3).

Within the tribe, I was immediately drawn to Rodger Bingham, who quickly became known as "Kentucky Joe" because of another contestant's quick wit. Rodger and I felt like father and daughter from the start, and we soon began spending quality time together. We spent most of our shared minutes doing tasks that needed to be done. In the midst of a game where it was every player for himself or herself by the end, Rodger put the needs of others first.

Selflessly, he took the outside position of our sardine-can sleeping setup. He knew that was the coldest, draftiest place of all and that he would benefit the least by offering us the best, which was between two other breathing warm bodies. He offered the best to the rest of us, and he offered that early and often. He was never the first to eat, almost always the last.

Rodger taught me how to fish and how to build a fire. And by his quiet, steady company and instructions, Rodger taught me that although we were all the way out in the outback, we were never so far that we would outrun, outwit, outplay, or outlast the blessings and protection of our mighty God. Rodger pointed my eyes, through our alliance in heart, to reliance on faith. When we could call on nothing else, we called on His name. We prayed—right there, out loud, pouring out our hearts. Every night and morning we prayed, beginning with praising God and thanking Him, praying for our families back home, and asking for safety in the long, uncertain days that lay ahead of us.

While my survival item, the headdress, was solely mine, Rodger's survival item became a survival item for all of us. Rodger brought his Bible. On many a night, that book saved us from worry, transgressions, and fear. Rodger opened my eyes to what fellowship could look like on the other side of a planet. Our *alliance* with one another was built on our *reliance* on God.

There were many nights when sleep was unattainable due to cold and rocky ground. If at any point during the day a person's gear got wet, and he or she did not get it to a hot sunny rock to dry, the person slept wet. We all learned quickly that the hotter the temperature was during the day, the colder it was at night. Wet clothes and socks and shoes and a cold night did not add up to a good night's sleep. But having Rodger on our team was more of a blessing than I can express. His obedience to a faithful God helped all of us. Despite sleeping right on the ground, with bumps and rocks and spiders and snakes, he helped us close our eyes with hope and a little more comfort each night. We had a shelter to sleep in and scriptures to rest on.

This verse became my song: "Finally, brothers and sisters, whatever is true, whatever is noble, whatever is right, whatever is pure, whatever is lovely, whatever is admirable—if anything is excellent or praiseworthy—think about such things" (Philippians 4:8). It would make its way back to me in future times of trouble. Ultimately, it is a song of gratitude and of fixing my eyes on what is from above and not on the wind or the water below, as Peter did in Matthew 14:29–32. Focusing on what has been done *for* you can keep you from sinking in what is happening *to* you at the time.

Despite sharing real estate with nine-tenths of the world's deadliest snakes, my ability to feel safe was made possible by faith and by fellowship. God knew I needed a trusted outback buddy, and I am forever grateful for all He showed me through my time with Rodger. To this day, the two of us keep in touch, and I pray that everyone who hears his name or encounters him knows what a heart he has for God and for others, how much fear he conquered, and how much he sacrificed for me in a game in which the only way to win is to be the last one standing.

Jump!

There were many challenges in *Survivor*. One in particular called us to retrieve a crate of survival supplies beneath the water and swim down a river with it to dry land. The first team to successfully bring their crate to land won the supplies. But there was a catch. In order to get to the crate, we had to first jump off a roughly fifty-foot-high cliff, swim to the right spot, and then dive down as a team to unlock it from a chain. I wish I had been the person who could not wait to jump! I wish that then, or even now, jumping seemed exciting. I hated that the game runners seemed to be always making us jump off something or out of something.

My strong distaste for the notion of jumping off a cliff paled in com-

parison to Rodger's fear. He did not know how to swim. That day I
didn't jump because I wanted to win; I jumped because I knew that if I
were in the water already, I could make sure Rodger was okay when he
jumped. I wanted to be in the water with him when he got there. Sometimes you have to get in the water with people to help them get through
their fears.

After I took the leap, I felt the surface of the water hit my skin pain-
fully, and plugging my nose did nothing to stop water from breaking into
every corner of my body. I plunged so far down that it took an uncom-
fortably long time to reach the surface. But I was there, looking back and
up for my friend.

Rodger was next. He jumped. And as my tears met the water, all that
liquid ran together. He jumped and he swam. I don't even remember if we
won or lost the challenge that day, but I know that Roger was victorious,
and it was one of the most teachable moments yet in my life. Jumping
required faith, and swimming requires trust. Rodger had both. I would
have done anything to help him conquer that challenge in the water. After
all, he had already become my life preserver on land.

On Dry Land

The days in the outback were long. And each day that took us farther
away from our original ration portion of rice felt longer. We spent several
hours of every day gathering sticks for fire, tending the fire, looking for a
branch and some twine to make a fishing rod, and searching for bait. Trying to find crickets for bait was one of the most challenging things to do
on a starving stomach, with muscles in various stages of atrophy after a
night of sleeping not a wink. It was as though the crickets were mocking
how slow we were. Our bodies were feeding on themselves, and our bodily

engines were not able to get out of first gear. Once we conquered a cricket for bait, we tied it to a homemade hook and hoped to catch a fish.

Do you know how many fish I caught in the thirty-nine days of *Survivor*? Zero. I did manage to pull up a couple of turtles one day. Catching a turtle was the best moment—then the worst moment—ever. Feeling the tug on the line and reeling it up, only to find out that I caught something I could not eat was so disappointing. Turtles were a protected species, so when I caught one, I had to throw it back. I was so hungry I would have eaten the shell if possible. That same day, I felt another pull on my line and—another turtle. That time, the motion of drawing it out of the water made me pass right out! This was not good news for anyone who wanted to stick around the *Survivor* game.

Catching a fish was important for two reasons: it meant having food, and it gave a contestant insurance against being voted off. The person who came back with fish was surely safe, as those who could fish successfully were necessary on their teams. I worked hard to learn to do it, but I was terrible at it. What kept me in the game, despite my inability to catch fish and the fact that my knot-tying skills were no longer as important as they once were, was working hard, being a good teammate, helping out, encouraging my teammates, and staying out of troublesome conversations. Being a good teammate in the Australian outback was no different from being a good teammate at work in the States, on a softball field, or in a dugout. I loved my tribe, and they were family away from family.

Without clocks or watches, the sun was our guide for time. Every third day or so we seemed to face a challenge in which our team and the other would compete. Each time we met, we found out which member from the tribe that lost the previous challenge had been voted off. Every time we faced off, the remaining tribe members looked fainter, weaker, and much more visibly exhausted than before.

At the close of each challenge, the victorious tribe claimed the prize, which was often a bit of food and occasionally some supplies we needed. At that point, the team prizes were essential for survival, and we appreciated them because they motivated us and kept our spirits up. We did our best, and when the number of members in each tribe got down to four, we merged.

This is where things got a little sticky, as our tribe had bonded as a unit, and the other team seemed to have a plan to wipe out our members. The only way to guarantee survival was to win the personal challenges and maintain a majority over the other tribe. The intensity and strategy ramped up. I never won an individual challenge. Not once. That was frustrating and disheartening, but I now thank God for that time of facing discouragement, as I know He was growing me closer to Him. So I rested on Him and Him alone—fully. He would not waste my pain, hunger, or frustration.

When the Time Was Right

To this day, hearing the notes of the *Survivor* music makes my heart skip a beat. Once my season on the game was complete, I wish I understood why, at the time, I wanted to run away from this period in my life that would be so pivotal.

Part of me wanted to lock away the whole experience. Quite frankly, life changed course so rapidly and so enormously after the show that I did not have time to look back and reflect on the fact that it did certainly not *de*fine me, but it sure did *re*fine me.

I watched our season when it first aired in 2001. Then it was seventeen years before I wanted to watch it again. Finally, for my fortieth birthday, I was ready to see what I had done in the outback. Tim and I found the DVDs and watched the show with the kids. They were old enough to understand it—and I was finally ready to relive it.

No doubt, being on *Survivor* changed me. One biblical truth that was impressed so firmly on my heart as a result of my time in the outback is John 15:5, when Jesus says, "I am the vine; you are the branches. If you remain in me and I in you, you will bear much fruit; apart from me you can do nothing."

The outback revealed to me God's wonderful creations in a way I had never seen—the kangaroo, the wallaby, the open sky, the sounds of night. I started my Australian adventure as a young girl desperate to see what I was made of without the availability of anything that would comfort me. It was a chapter in my life that I tucked into my heart as a time of growing deeply in my faith. God made clear to me that I did not need to be away from anyone who cared about me to know what I was made of because He had specifically placed in my life all those I missed back home—the ones who were on my mind with every beat of my heart while in Australia—to love me and for me to love.

I may have gone into that adventure to find out who I was without all the comforts of those I love around me, but by the time I left, I realized whose I am and how He had blessed and would continue to bless me with the most incredible hearts since then. God showed me that I did not ever want to be away from Tim again, that my family was my support, and that He was my portion. He showed me that even in the middle of a desert, in the rough places, He is there, He has gone before me, and He will never let me go. I learned that grit and grace do not have to be mutually exclusive. God opened my eyes to see clearly that I am made by *Him,* that apart from Him I can do nothing, that *He* is my comforter, and that He is never away from me. "I say to myself, '*The* LORD *is my portion;* therefore I will wait for him'" (Lamentations 3:24, emphasis added).

5

Surviving Hot Topics

❧

That is why, for Christ's sake, I delight in weaknesses, in insults, in hardships, in persecutions, in difficulties. For when I am weak, then I am strong.

—2 Corinthians 12:10

S hortly after *Survivor,* in an attempt to get back to the *real* reality of life and get my days back on pace, I returned to design work and took a position working for Steven Monti, my former mentor in footwear design. During that winter of 2001, my winnings from *Survivor* helped me take care of some college loans and let me feel what freedom from debt could be like for the first time in a while. Facing the reality of future expenses, I was content getting back into the swing of things with a regular job when an offer came to me by mail. It was from the Style Network, a brand of E! Networks, which was looking for a designer to host a show about styling on a budget called *The Look for Less.* I had to admit I was curious about the opportunity, but I was still a little shell-shocked from the television aspect of *Survivor* and desperately wanted to get back to normal. What I could not see, and was not prepared to accept as God's gift at the time, was that *normal* would not be part of my future. *Survivor* had changed normal for me forever.

In his book *Ordering Your Private World,* Gordon MacDonald talks about train tracks and how the turntable can redirect a train. He remembers his grandmother saying, "I think God has a round table too. He uses it to change the pathway of people He's calling to serve him. . . . His round table will send you off in a different direction." The switch, which can be in only one position or the other, determines the track and direction of a train. That's exactly what *Survivor* did for me. It was a track shift. There was a certain track of life behind me, and I was looking to get back on it after the show. Though at some point it became clear that the tracks had shifted, it was not clear to me *who* had shifted them. The one thing I was sure of was that the destination had changed. Nothing from this juncture would be something I had ever envisioned. Nothing would look like the plans I had laid out for my life. Looking back on the actual adventure of *Survivor* was exhilarating at times, but at other times, I lay awake at night wondering, *What did I just do to my life?* I had to decide to readjust my point of view to see the moments that came along as invitations and opportunities that would not have come before I took that leap into the outback.

The offer from *The Look for Less* was an invitation to a new kind of work, and I had let the letter sit unanswered on my desk so long that I pretty much counted myself out of it. Relying on the manners with which my parents raised me, I called E! and thanked them for thinking of me for the position. I went on to say that I was sure they had found a host for the job by that time. I appreciated the invitation, I told them, and concluded by saying I was sorry to have missed the audition.

There, I thought, *I can go back to life as it was.*

Not so fast.

The person on the other end of the phone said, "We have not filled the spot yet, and we would love to fly you out business class to meet with the team. We will put you up in a hotel in West LA." I had never been offered a flight to a job interview before, and the offer certainly helped me decide to honor their request!

I chose an outfit the way I always did—creatively and on a dime. This one cost eleven dollars and ninety cents from H&M. After I met with the team wearing a budget-conscious "look for less," they offered me the job. The salary was more than I could earn as a freelancer or even as a salaried designer at the time, and it sounded almost too good to be true. Keeping in mind that this was an opportunity God had given me, I accepted that job and began hosting *The Look for Less*. I traveled all over the United States to just about every mall in America, including the Mall of America in Minnesota, where we re-created certain runway looks for a hundred dollars or less in less than an hour!

Considering that *Survivor* would not exactly count as training in television, this was a job where I learned the hard way every single day. Looking and talking into a camera, memorizing hosting wraps, takes and retakes, and working with a tight-knit camera and sound crew that gave me comforting smiles when I felt totally out of my element became my new reality.

Amid the adjustment to this new role and to the travel it required, in addition to still being Tim's top fan while he played football at Boston College, being in the sky provided a great metaphor for life. I felt very much up in the air—every week a new city, a big game for Tim, wondering where my new career direction would go and where his dream of playing in the NFL would take him.

One thing I knew: wherever our careers would take us, we would go together. Tim, like a true quarterback, could see ahead enough to call a big play to ensure that our game plan would be successful.

Tim had mentioned liking a certain pair of shoes, and I was so excited to get them for him for his birthday that year. I had planned on making a big deal of "his next steps in the next year," as a big step would be heading into the NFL selections. I remember hiding the shoes as we headed into Boston for a night to celebrate. I had even lined up a couple of his friends to surprise him at a restaurant. All that remained in my plan was to give him those navy shoes. He was going to love them! But the surprise was on me.

Tim, strangely intent about not heading out to meet his friends just yet, was beginning to ruin the carefully laid plans I had been working on. All I wanted was to see him take some steps in his new shoes, and all he wanted was to get on one knee.

On his birthday, he knelt on the bridge across the Charles River in Boston, Massachusetts, and proposed. In that moment, everything came to a halt in the best way as I shouted over the bridge down to the rowers in the Charles that I was going to "marry Tim!" The very thing I had hoped would come once we knew what the future held became what held us through all the changes in cities and jobs and through all the ups and downs to come. The promise and covenant before God to be with one another before, during, and after it all was the most pivotal moment of my life. Neither of us knew what the future held. I was giving this new hosting thing a shot, and Tim was about to finish his last year of Boston College. Yet nothing mattered more than being together through whatever would come our way. I began that night as a girl with a pair of blue shoes wrapped to give my boyfriend and ended it with a promise that all the steps he would take in them would be with me by his side.

Eighteen months later, Tim began his career in the NFL, playing with the Philadelphia Eagles, and in July 2002, we took our vows and became husband and wife in my home state of Rhode Island. Instead of cutting cake, we scooped ice cream cones—our favorite dessert and date treat. We danced to our wedding song, "When You Say Nothing at All" by Alison Krauss. To this day on our anniversary, I get into my wedding dress and veil, and we dance to it—and time stands still.

During the first year of our marriage, we made Manhattan Beach, California, our off-football-season home, and we rented a small apartment on the top floor of a house owned by a sweet couple who lived below. I worked in the headquarters of the E! News offices, and it made sense to be there—until it didn't make sense. Before long, Tim had been cut by the Philadelphia Eagles, and I realized the team at *The Look for Less* was going to look for another host. Tim was out of a job, and it looked like I would be out of a job too, so we found ourselves in "What is the next wise thing to do?" mode.

"Darling"

Several people mentioned to me that ABC's daytime talk show, *The View*, was looking for a new cohost because Lisa Ling was leaving to pursue something new. I was familiar with the show and said to myself, *Well, I spend the first part of that show talking back to the screen from this side, and it would be more satisfactory to actually tell those women in person that there is another way to see the issues they discuss!*

Before I had much time to start imagining what being part of *The View* would be like, my broadcasting agent called and told me that I could get on a call with the show's executive producer. Following that talk, and once they had an idea of my political leanings at the time, I was invited to come and join a search for the person who would eventually fill the chair. A number of women would be up for the job.

This felt big to me. It felt important. And in a way, it felt the same as *Survivor* did, meaning that although it was nothing I was specifically qualified for, I felt called to at least explore the opportunity. I was not a political expert; I was just a shoe designer who loved shopping on a budget and who loved my husband, God, country, country music, family, and football. I was fairly certain I would not get the spot, but I also thought, *How could I turn down getting to work next to Barbara Walters for a week?*

The adventure took me to New York City and to a room at a pretty nice hotel. I checked in and giggled to myself when they told me I would be staying in room 2020.

Like 20/20? *Barbara's legendary news program! Perfect vision! This is so meant to be,* I thought.

The next day I prepared and prayed and picked my outfit. My mother-in-law, Betsy, who is one of my very best friends in the whole world, helped me prepare not only by helping me decide what I would wear but also preparing me with the armor of the Word of God in a Bible she and Tim's dad, Don (I call him "Big D"), had given me. Regardless of the topic slated for the show, I knew my first bit of research had to begin in that big book each morning. The pressure was there but not without the protection and provision that came from our families' prayers.

The next thing I knew, I was at the table with the ladies of *The View,* as they were called. After a round of hot topics that had me bare my heart about a few key issues, the team from the show sent me back to the hotel. Following a hunt through Times Square for a gluten-free snack (since I had recently found out that celiac disease was the root of my tummy issues all these years), I returned to the hotel. There I learned that I had made it to the next round, which would involve three days or more at the Hot Topics table. It was like two parts *Survivor* and one part Boston College softball tryout. My adrenaline shot through the roof! Between my ability to outlast and my walk-on way, I was ready. For the next three days, I sat at the Hot Topics table and had the chance to talk about issues from my perspective again. Also, an interview with Hillary Clinton went fairly well, and I left the office of ABC feeling a calm assurance that even if I did not get the job, I had overcome the uncertainty about my skill and learned something new.

On the third day, as I sat in my hotel room eating a protein bar after the show, the phone rang. I answered and heard the unmistakable voice of Barbara Walters: "Darling, it's Barbara Walters calling. You have the job. Congratulations. The chair is yours."

No one except my mother had ever called me "darling." The difference was that my mom said it jokingly, and Barbara said it *not* jokingly. It was her word. Every email she has sent me since then begins with it, and almost every sentence she has ever spoken has as well. Elegance and authority came with the word, and I felt both immediately.

Getting the job on *The View* was more of a shock than being cast on *Survivor*. Once I hung up the phone, I jumped up and down on the bed and screamed. I could not have been more excited! This was amazing news from the pioneer herself, Barbara Walters!

In the Hot Seat

Once I was hired, Tim and I planned our move from the West Coast to the East Coast, from Los Angeles to New York City. About the same time, Tim signed with the Washington Redskins. The distance from New York to Washington, DC, was commutable but not easy for us. We were trying to be there for each other while living apart, and I joined Tim for all his games. The weekdays seemed to last forever, and I missed him terribly.

On one of the first weekends after getting the job, I had been anticipating traveling to see Tim play his first start with the Redskins. I *had* to be there and finished up *The View* just in time to get out of NYC and head to him. I missed him. The week was long, and there was something comforting to me about watching him play and seeing his dreams realized.

I remember telling him at one point that we would go wherever he

played, that his career in the NFL was always the priority in our family—
and that we could do the commute. Long-distance relationships were not
foreign to us, and we had built our communication and relationship muscles during his last year in college, during *Survivor,* and when he was
playing for a brief time in Berlin, Germany.

The day of his first start with the Redskins, I was more excited for his
new job than for mine! Watching him excel, knowing how much film he
had studied, and realizing how much time he put into learning the offense in a condensed period made my heart beat. After the game, we celebrated the opportunity and thanked God for it. That night, we had to
drive from the game through the night and through Times Square at
2:00 a.m. in a black pickup truck just to make it to our hotel in time for
me to shower and get to my job. This became our rhythm for the next two
years. Then the New York Giants picked him up, and we were in the same
city for the first time since we were newly married!

My first week on *The View* was pleasant, but during the second week,
I began to feel as out of place as our pickup truck looked in New York
City. Once the celebration of a new host and the introductions and
friendly welcomes were under our belts, the gloves came off.

I was raised in a home where we lovingly talked about and tackled
issues, and it was a home where we could and were encouraged to see
things from another's perspective. Perhaps that happened because my father is a visionary and an architect, and he loved to try to see all the angles
on a subject. And my mother, a brilliant attorney, was trained in examin-
ing what the other side of a story might look like. Ours was a home where
no one had to see everything the same way in the process of discussion,
and no one was punished for bringing another point to the table. The
table at *The View* was a little more . . . *charged.*

Technically, my new job was the easiest thing to do. I arrived at work at 9:00 each weekday morning, got my makeup done, and had my hair styled. Someone picked out my outfit and my shoes. Someone else did research on the celebrity guests for the day and handed it to me. Then I was supposed to begin by discussing the hot topics of the day with some girlfriends.

The reality is, it was the most "difficult-easy" job I've ever had. Have you ever had one of those? They are baffling because the unfortunate, unnecessary, manufactured stressful surroundings exponentially negate the blessing of the comforts.

The View was *the* hot spot for celebrities and heads of state alike. Tom Cruise or Denzel Washington would come by, and current and former presidents of the United States would be our guests, and we shared the morning talking together. Sometimes we made awesome meals with Paula Deen, Bobby Flay, Rachael Ray, or the Pioneer Woman, Ree Drummond. The cutest dogs from the Westminster Kennel Club Dog Show paraded about. We could hear people in the audience clapping for us (well, they didn't always clap for me), and we had an entire crew of trained and skilled technicians and artists whose job was to make us look and sound as good as possible to one million people during the hour, every day of the week.

Oprah would drop by and we would get a hug, and then maybe we could chat with the latest Olympic gold medalists. We also got to talk about and talk with Justin Timberlake and Beyoncé, and have the privilege of expressing our opinions and discussing them with friends over coffee. LL Cool J, Prince, and Justin Bieber, who raced me on a Segway one morning for a segment, would be in our offices on any given day. Paul McCartney, the Kardashians, the Clintons, the Obamas, and the Romneys made multiple appearances on the show. With generals, politicians, actors, animals, and athletes, our offices were bustling each day with the most interesting people and stories. I stand beyond grateful to have been a part of a group of women who could holistically and wholeheartedly bare our souls and take on tough issues people were "not supposed to talk about"—abortion, politics, marriage, religion. Sadly, there were times too when not every opinion was respected and our discussion at the table sounded more like a catfight than a smart debate. I regret that in the thick of those moments we were sending women a message about how difficult it could sometimes be to have good, deep, disagreeing conversations. Yet we all did our best.

Eventually, I settled into the routine. Debating between eleven and eleven thirty, eastern time, every weekday morning became my routine for ten years.

A Lone Voice

Barbara Walters had a brilliant vision for *The View*—to bring together women from different generations, different backgrounds, and different political spheres to discuss hot topics. Looking back now, I see that I should have been able to deduce, based on the title of the program, precisely what I would be getting into if I applied for the job and actually got it. The show was not called *The Views* or *Different Views* or *Honoring One Another's Views*. It was called *The View*, as in definitive and singular. Yes, there were bonds of friendship formed around the table despite opposing views, but there were also bonds broken because of those differing perspectives.

As uncomfortable as it was for me at times to be the lone voice for some issues I was not qualified to take on, my invitation and calling to be there were clear to me, though what was ahead was not. This was a place where I walked in as a newlywed twentysomething with a design degree—the same girl who had missed the 2000 election because she was in the Australian outback and who had never spoken a word about politics aloud or been in a debate before this *ever*.

It all seemed crazy to me, but it got crazier as I had all three of my babies. With each one, *The View* would celebrate with me, and we would throw fun showers for the audience. The real connection I felt was with other women, and I loved knowing I was not alone when it came to parenting and working—and trying to make it all "work." When each of my children was born, *The View* provided a *Lion King* moment at the end of the six-week maternity leave—which Barbara fought to get approved for me each time—where my new baby and I would walk out and make our first television appearance together. It makes me laugh and tear up at the same time. There is nothing better than having your joy shared.

Debating hot topics on television after being up at night with a newborn, or caring for toddlers with the croup or a tummy bug and then pumping breast milk is not advised. Side effects include incomplete thoughts and sentences, frazzled moments, and lots of mistakes along the way.

I look back now on my years at *The View* and all the opportunities it gave me. There was President George W. Bush's private invitation to visit the Oval Office with our whole family. The visit included the unique blessing of sitting there and talking with the president of the United States while he helped wrangle my little Taylor, who was running around the room. Memories include speaking on behalf of breast cancer funding at the Republican National Convention and interviewing President Barack Obama four times. I am full of gratitude (and still a little shocked when I see pictures of it all) for the opportunities God permitted in my life. I do believe that I earned the equivalent of a master's degree in broadcasting with Barbara Walters as my professor. Nothing could have prepared me for the experience, so I prepared my heart each morning with the armor of God (see Ephesians 6:10–18) because I knew each day would have its challenges.

I can say without hesitation that my decade at *The View* strengthened my mind, refined my citizen's heart, and sharpened my skill. And the in-betweens were a lot of fun. Politically outnumbered, I made it my goal (calling on my *Survivor* skills) to hold the torch for the "other side" and outlast the backlash as long as I could endure. As small as my lone voice felt in that arena, I trusted that God had a purpose planted in it.

6

Not Surviving *The View*

I used to be afraid of failing at something that really mattered to me, but now I'm more afraid of succeeding at things that don't matter.

—BOB GOFF

Typically, I did not close the door to my office at *The View*. The hallway ended where my office door was, and the wall had a window, which made me feel like I had a window in my office. I joked to anyone who decided to visit me that I had "a corner window office." I loved the quiet, cozy location and made the office mine over the years. I even put black-and-white buffalo-check wallpaper on a focus wall so I could really settle into my office. Shoes lined one wall, and the rest of the office was, well, a mess, mainly because I did not stay there and hang out each day, as the hours leading up to the on-air portion of the job took their toll on me. I wanted to get home to Grace, Taylor, and Isaiah as quickly as possible.

Immediately following the show, we would have our postshow meeting and spend some time talking to our producers, many of whom I am still friends with. I was usually all talked out by the time our postshow meetings came to a close anyway, after arriving at nine in the morning, getting filled in on everyone's personal life and family, laughing, yelling, and participating in debates-before-the-debate. Like a fighter after ten rounds in a ring, I was exhausted from holding one side of the issue alone, though happy to do it, and I needed the faces of my kids to be close to mine as soon as possible.

By March 2013, ten years after I first got the job, things had begun to feel unusual. There was a lot of guest hosting going on. I remember Brooke Shields coming in with a team of assistants and studying the topics really hard in the makeup chair, going over notes with an effort that seemed, well, familiar. I remember the instant I thought, *Wait a minute!* And it dawned on me: Brooke was not just guest hosting; she was *applying* for a job. My gut instincts had been telling me that some-one was going to be joining the show, and those instincts were being proven daily.

Days later, Maria Menounos came with the same intentionality Brooke had. Something was going on. *Someone is going to be added to the table.* I asked my producer directly if that was the case, and he assured me it was not.

Still, I felt unsettled. There was something unspoken and uncomfort-able when I would greet the sweet women who joined the show on certain days: an awkward hello, a hesitant glance at their notes, a deep breath when I would leave—as if they had something to tell me but could not. Typically, when someone was an occasional guest host, it was a way to promote a book or a show or it was just for fun. That month, I sensed something different was going on.

By the time Maria Menounos came, I was pretty sure I had figured out what was happening, and I remember saying to her, "Look, from what I can gather, I think they are replacing me. Tell them your parents' story. Tell them your story. Don't hold back. Tell them who you are. Go get this thing." Shocked, she looked at me and smiled a knowing smile. I knew she could not say anything, but that did not mean I would not wish her well.

The next week calmed down a bit in terms of visitors, and I actually began to think I was just being paranoid about someone taking my job.

Then came the knock on my office door.

When I opened it, not one but two male figures stood there—the producer of *The View* and an ABC executive.

"We would like to speak with you about something," one of them said.

Without emotion, without wasting a minute, they told me they were not renewing my contract. They said the show would be going in a less political direction, and that I could leave that day or the next day or stay for the remainder of this current season—but, come September, they were replacing me.

I could not breathe—literally, could not breathe.

Gasping, I asked permission to get my inhaler and, after fumbling around the mess of my office (asking myself why I couldn't have cleaned up that morning so it would have been easier to find the thing), took a puff, then another. I was bent over—shock, asthma, and betrayal all stealing my wind.

"I'm really thankful for all the years here" were the first words that came out of my mouth.

I should have been more thankful before, even when it was hard. But I sure was thankful in that moment, when my job and the whole experience on *The View* was being taken away.

The next thing I said was, "Why?"

"What could I have done?" I continued. "Was there something I could have done differently? Can I do something differently now? If you would just tell me, I would work on that—and make it better."

Again, I pleaded, "Was there something I could have done differently?" I kept asking, trying to figure out how to get it back, trying to get it all back.

But it is almost always impossible to get back what is not yours to begin with.

"There is nothing you could have done," they informed me. "Are you going to be okay?"

I looked up at their stoic faces. One cared, at least a little bit. The other was likely questioning whether an ambulance would be needed and what kind of publicity that would get for the show. In a moment of what must have been self-soothing, I repeated, "I'll be okay. I'll be okay."

I followed those words with an outpouring of confusion: "I just don't understand why. What did I do wrong? I have come here and had babies and shared my heart. I have done my work, and I just don't understand. Why did you not tell me there was something I could have done better, so I could have done that?" Blank stares met those anguished words.

"I'll be okay," I repeated and wheezed.

The men backed out of the room, and I shut the door behind them. I sat alone in my office for about an hour and a half sobbing, just sobbing. Feeling a dose of betrayal and a whopper of confusion, I felt like the walls of the building were folding in on me.

The day the two men knocked on my office door, I had to fly to California for an assignment. I cried all the way to the airport, called Tim, and sobbed more. Then I cried the entire flight, on a plane that seemed to circumnavigate the globe, under the flight-brand blanket. It was so soaked that I could not bear to leave it there.

The day I heard that *The View* would not renew my contract, my career world fell apart, and it fell apart because it was mine. That was the problem. It was not *all* mine, but it certainly was not all *His* yet. That would require surrender. And surrender was not something I knew how to do yet.

God used that time after *The View* released me to instruct me in not alliance (reliance on others) and in not me-liance (reliance on myself) but in total reliance on Him.

People often ask me if I would rather return to the Australian outback on *Survivor* or to the Hot Topics table at *The View*. Hmm. Thirty-nine days without enough food and without familiar friends, keeping company with nine out of the world's ten deadliest snakes? Or sitting at a table with other women who felt as passionately about their views as I did about mine—only they agreed with each other, and I had to stand my ground by myself? To this day, the question of which intense situation I would prefer remains a theoretical toss-up, as both were wonderfully rewarding and fiercely challenging. In both situations, this girl had no idea what she had just gotten herself into. The selection of snacks in the green room at *The View* might cause me to lean toward choosing that over *Survivor*, but as I mentioned, it's still a toss-up. Regardless of the answer, I am thankful for each opportunity, and I grew deeper in my walk with God in each place. "Getting passed by can feel like a great injury. But it's not," Bob Goff says in *Love Does*. I had never seen it that way. Until now.

Leaving Well

Being asked to go when you want to stay hurts. And asking what to do to make it better and getting no response hurts. When *The View* did not renew my contract for the following seasons as planned, I initially wanted to just walk out those doors in March, but my agreement provided that I could stay and get paid through August. No stay, no pay. So I stayed as long as I could. The chair at the Hot Topics table was mine for the remainder of my contract that year, and I was not ready to give them that too. I knew that staying would be difficult, but I also knew I would be able to tough it out. I knew I would show them that I was not going to leave easily, but what I did not know was that in that time God would teach me to see what it looked like to leave well. *The View* had let me go, but I was sure that this great God did not and would not let me go.

I stood firm in confidence that He would give me strength to continue to go to work and do my best each day. I may have been fired, but in the wake of that, God gave me the gift of being inspired with gratitude for all I had experienced during those ten years within the walls of ABC.

One morning, standing in my kitchen, this scripture was on my mind: "Give thanks in all circumstances; for this is God's will for you in Christ Jesus" (1 Thessalonians 5:18).

All circumstances? I asked myself. Yes, that is what God was instructing. So I gave it a try. I prayed—deeply. I prayed thanks, thanking God for the chance to work at *The View,* thanking Him for His provision, thanking Him in advance for the next job He would have for me, praying again that I could keep going into work as long as He wanted me in that building, and asking Him to help me stay joyful even in the midst of a storm.

During that time, God gave me a gift I will never forget. He gave me the gift of leaving well. That which was required was not of me and was all from Him. Left to myself, I would not leave well at all. Left to my own, I would likely try but fail. Leaving would not go well in my own power because I had less than what the situation called for. I was feeling betrayed, hurt, exhausted, and sad—all of which paved the way to burning bridges, not leaving well.

Leaving well required strength, strength that had to come from God because I had none of my own. Showing up every day and working hard for a team, knowing I had been fired and replaced—yet still putting my heart out there and voicing my minority opinions—was not easy. Leaving well did not always feel like it was going well.

As I passed people in the hallways and as they dropped by my office feeling bad for me and knowing I would soon be gone, I told them, "I love you. But you are not invited into a pity party, because I am not throwing myself one."

Some days work was so uncomfortable I wanted to leave that very minute. One day, I remembered one of the *Survivor* challenges in the Australian outback. In a game called Perch, we had to stand on a log in the river longer than anyone else, through rain and storms and heat and hunger. There on that perch I stood for more than eight and a half hours. The lesson I learned is that whatever your log is, stay on it as long as you can, but get off before someone kicks you off. At *The View,* I knew there would have to be a time to get off, but that time had not yet come. I was determined to outlast the nonrenewal of my contract as long as I could with gratitude and with God directing my heart.

God gave me peace and opened my eyes in so many ways between the time I found out I was leaving and when I actually left. He also gave me enough freedom and light to walk with hope, not dread. He gifted me with fortitude to remain strong in my voice at the very table where the chair was no longer mine and where my hot topics opinions mattered less than ever to those sitting around me.

In addition, I felt as though God lit up a billboard showing me the unique gifts those around me brought to the table each day and allowing me to express my gratitude for those individuals. As I chose thankfulness, I became increasingly determined to let everyone know how much they meant to me. I remember saying to one, "You are really gifted at product segments. I need you to know that," and to another, "You make the most

incredible notes for movie segment interviews." Thankfulness left no
room for pity. I couldn't feel sorry for myself and feel grateful for others at
the same time.

By Friday of each week, I was tired of being fired. Being in a position
where I was being replaced was stressful. Yet God gave me enough of what
I needed—but not more than I needed—to fall into His arms at the close
of each week and beg for more strength. He was my portion. The idea of
daily bread became impressed upon my heart. *God, give me just enough
to get through this day. But not so much that I don't need You.*

He did just that. Because He is my enough.

When I walked through the halls of ABC with my head down, God
lifted it up and held it high. Psalm 3:3 became so real to me: "But you,
LORD, are a shield around me, my glory, the One who lifts my head high."
I felt that shield around me each day as I walked to my office, the very last
door anyone could find, and the walk for the first time seemed a mile too
long.

What used to be my refuge—the safe place, the office tucked away
from all the drama—no longer belonged to me. Perhaps that is precisely
what God wanted me to see, that it never was mine to begin with; it was
always His.

I stood firm in my job as long as I could. When I went home each
day, I packed up one or two items from my decade-long collection of *View*
memorabilia, things I would not want to leave behind just in case that day
happened to be the last day I could stand on the log.

This season of my life proved to be the most trying professional time
I faced until that point. And I still had to keep my wits about me to take
on topics on which I was far outnumbered and then return home after an
hour commute to be a cheery mom to children who needed my joy. I was
getting worn down. I was worn down with pretending that everything

was okay when it really wasn't. I was fatigued, trying to have a good attitude about being let go, still debating topics at the table, now searching for whatever other opportunities might be available, and still being a good mom and wife.

At the end of one particular week that got the best of me, I looked sad when I got home, and our kids noticed. "Why are you sad, Mommy?" they asked.

"Well," I answered, "Mommy was told a little while ago that they are not renewing my contract at work."

"What does that mean?" one wanted to know.

"It means Mommy is . . . It means Mommy is fired," I explained.

"What does fired mean?" one asked.

"It means they don't want me to come to work there anymore. They have someone else to do my job."

"Why?" one asked again.

"I don't know."

"Did you do something wrong?" one wanted to know.

"I don't think so. I mean, I am not perfect, but I did not know I was doing anything wrong. And I wish that if I had been doing something wrong, they had told me so I could have worked on it and done better. I did my best, and I feel good about that."

Beginning to understand, the kids had more questions: "So you don't have a job there anymore?" and "They are giving your job to someone else?" and "Do you know that person?"

"No, I don't know the person," I said, "but I am going to tell her to do her best."

"Why?"

"Because it is the right thing to do. That is why."

"Are you sad?" one of the kids wanted to know.

"Yes, very sad," I admitted.

"I'm sorry, Mommy. I'm sorry you got fired," said Grace.

"I'm sorry, Mommy. I'm sorry you are sad," said Taylor.

"Sorry, Mommy. So sorry, Mommy," Isaiah added.

Hugs like I really needed enveloped me.

"It will be okay, lovies," I told them. Speaking those words aloud seemed to help me as much as it helped them in that moment.

In the midst of all this, I was also trying to secure my next job. Tim was my support. He assured me that I did not have to stress about finding something right away. As much as I am sure he was relieved to know I would no longer be in the crosshairs of that Hot Topics table again, he knew I loved to work hard there. He knew I felt a mission there, and he knew God was asking me to do what I was doing. He was the rock I leaned and rested on when things got crazy. "We will be okay," he said to me. "God has this."

I wished I could have zoomed through the door of our home at the end of each of those long weeks and asked the kids what kind of cookies they wanted to make from scratch and then played flag football without missing a beat. But I did miss beats. Because I was beat. My kids saw a mommy who was sad, confused, disappointed, and rejected. But they did not see me dejected.

What is clear to me now is that in those moments of weakness, my kids were able to see resilience in me and to realize that things don't always go your way. In the weeks that followed, they witnessed me choose to trust that God was working for me, even when I had no work. They saw Mommy choose to see things through a thankful lens when I could, and they saw how that got me through one of the toughest times of my life. Over time, they saw me move from being fired to being inspired. We learned together that leaving well requires an attitude of gratitude. That gratitude brought into sight the "good" in goodbye.

Sometimes leaving happens on our own terms, and sometimes it doesn't. I believe deeply that in either situation it is possible to leave well. Here are some ways to do that:

Don't burn bridges. Romans 12:18 says, "If it is possible, as far as it depends on you, live at peace with everyone." There is no footnote to this verse that says to be at peace with others only when you have a job and are not being fired. God is asking this of us even in tough situations. Drop the matches and be a peacemaker. Discussing hot topics does not mean burning things or hearts along the way. Besides, you might be working with one of these individuals again someday.

Maintain contacts. Make sure you keep up by email or social media with the people who have impacted you. They have been a part of your life and might have insight about your next steps. Understand that you have been placed with these people for a reason, and know that the friendships made during your time with them are even more valuable than the work done.

Clean your office. I wish I were better at this. I left a few things behind, but my advice is to make sure that you leave the place in good shape for the next person. Maybe even leave a plant with a note, a new lamp, or set of pens. You are leaving, but someone else is arriving. Leave that person a present! You never know what it would mean to them.

Pray thanks in the departure. This was not easy for me. It required that I pray first that God make my heart grateful. Only He was able to do that. An attitude of gratitude is the key to a joyful departure. Try being thankful for three things each morning during the transition, and then leave the rest to God.

Leave no individuals unthanked for what they do each day. Tell everyone how they impacted you positively. Encourage them, even as you leave. Thank them for all they did for you.

Ask for recommendations and accept help. Ask your coworkers and bosses if they would put in a good word for you when needed.

Pass the Torch Well

Leaving well also requires passing the torch well, meaning to try to make the transition as easy as possible for the next person and to do as much as possible to set that person up for success.

One of the experiences *The View* gave me, which I will never forget, was carrying through the streets of New York City the official torch in celebration of the upcoming 2004 Olympic Games in Athens, Greece. Representing the United States of America and the Olympics was not something I took lightly.

On the morning of the big day, I climbed aboard a bus in Brooklyn, which took me to the place where I would receive the torch. I also received a pair of Olympic shorts and a T-shirt. Of course, I added a little flair to the outfit with an Olympic headband. All torchbearers were given an official Olympic torch from the games, one that had traveled the globe. Each time I hold it I get chills, and I have been known to run around my backyard, singing the national anthem and holding it, just for memory's sake.

The sense of history and significance I felt when I took the flame was overwhelming. Just thinking about the athletes and their pursuit of the Olympic goals was breathtaking in the best way.

Olympic torchbearers had the most important instruction and goal made quite clear: *Do not let the flame go out.* In order to keep the light bright and the flame lit, we all had to pass the torch well. Passing the torch well meant connecting effectively with the next person who would carry it. If the handoff was smooth, the torch was passed well. Because of the design of the torch, the person carrying it *had* to hold it upright—or the flame would go out. I conveyed to the next carrier the pointers I had heard about running with the torch: "Point the torch straight up. Watch your speed. Don't run too fast with it, and connect well with whomever is next. Thanks for letting me pass this to you! Go, USA!"

The honor of being at *The View* and sitting in arguably the hottest seat at the Hot Topics table was a torch worth passing well. I felt thankful that I was able to connect with Candace Cameron Bure and pass her the torch, along with all the advice and wisdom I had to offer, so she could carry the flame. Candace received that light well and held it upright and with great dignity and grace. She not only received the torch but made the seat at the Hot Topics table her own. She made it a place to shine the light on God's Word and His promises. She made the choice daily to draw the light. What we shared in common became an opportunity for the beginning of a fellowship and friendship between the two of us and a lesson in perspective.

When we are called to leave a place, even when it is not our choice, choosing to leave well and pass the torch well will be worth it.

7

Stealing Home and Mornings with Friends

The LORD himself goes before you and will be with you;
he will never leave you nor forsake you. Do not be afraid;
do not be discouraged.

—DEUTERONOMY 31:8

O ften in life we find ourselves between the bases, so to speak—
between jobs, decisions, relationships, goals, homes, or loca-
tions. This kind of transition is exactly where I was after my time at *The
View*. I did not want to wonder what would happen, so I took off running. Fast.

In baseball or softball, base runners customarily wait for the coach to
give the "go" or "steal" or "stay" signal to determine their steps. Sometimes they run ahead, asking that coach to bless their steps after they had
already decided to take them in an attempt to save the day, make a mark,
or do what was needed to get to the next base—with the best intentions.
I refer to this as "stealing home."

As my softball team's pinch runner, I had the opportunity to steal
bases and steal home quite often. In fact, as I mentioned earlier, all I did
for my team during the first two years of college was pinch run until I
finally earned a spot in the starting lineup. My job was to take the place
of the player who hit the ball and run fast, really fast, for her. Sometimes
my excitement, grit, and desire to impress my team and coaches—along
with a dose of pride—got in the way of smart base running. One incident
stands out from the rest.

It was a championship playoff game, the pressure was on, and our
Division I Big East team was positioned to take the title. One of our best

hitters smashed a line drive up the middle of the field and into the outfield for a double.

"Elisabeth! Get your helmet on!" yelled the coach.

I spit out my gum, pressed the foam of the helmet tight to my head, and said, "Yes, coach!" I raced to the field, then high-fived my teammate as we swapped places.

Carefully I watched my coach—one of the smartest I've ever had—go through the signals, hoping she would say she wanted me to steal. Much to my disappointment, she did not give me the sign.

With two outs, we were tied. I was in position to score the winning run. This was the moment when the benchwarming, walk-on pinch runner would win the game!

As the pitcher released the next pitch, I took my lead. The batter smacked the ball past the second baseman. I was going to score! Then I saw my coach hold up both hands high above her head with her palms facing me, telling me—what? To hold up at third base! *No way!* I was going home.

Our team had an unspoken rule: if you blow by a coach's hold, you better get yourself home, and you better be safe.

I was sure I could make it home, and I blew by her hold signal. On my way to stealing home, I thought, *This. Is. The. Moment. I. Have. Been. Waiting. For.*

I slid into home base only to be pounded by a catcher's glove—like an ax waiting for me. Screeching to a halt in a cloud of dusty infield clay, I heard the umpire roar, *"You are out!"*

The only thing worse than being called out was that this particular out ended our at-bat and gave the other team a chance to score. The only thing worse than that was that we lost the championship game and it was my fault. What was worse than that was the steam coming out of my coach's head and the fact that her eyes seemed to be on fire as she yelled, *"What the heck were you thinking?"*

The one person I was really trying to impress, so she would give me a starting job, was the one running at me—fully disappointed. She wanted me to score, just not right when I tried to do it. From where she stood, she could see better than I could, and she knew that the moment I chose to go was not the right time to go. It was the time to wait.

"That wasn't your base to steal!" she told me.

I have had other moments like that one, except they didn't involve a dusty uniform, smudged eye black, or a leg bruised by a catcher's glove. Instead, they involved making decisions boldly on my own power, in stressful times, and ignoring God's hold sign as I pressed on. They involved being called out when I was out of my league. They involved letting down someone, or everyone, who was counting on me. In all those situations, I was asking God to bless my steps while ignoring His sign to slow down at third.

Whatever it was, I went ahead and did it on my own. I had to, I thought; I wanted to, and I thought I could do it. It looked good, and it seemed possible—until it didn't.

A New Team

Years later, this walk-on pinch runner was hoping to save the day and win the game again, but I was not wearing cleats. It was after *The View* had not renewed my contract, and I was wearing heels. I needed to get myself a job. *The View* was behind me, and they had moved on. Finally, I was at peace with that—as long as I knew I had a spot somewhere else.

Not wanting to waste any time, I remembered that I had contact information for Roger Ailes, chairman and CEO of FOX News Channel.

When I had seen him in the past, he had casually mentioned that if I ever wanted to be at FOX, he had a place for me. Big times of need call for big risks, and contacting Roger Ailes was a big risk for me. *Will he remember what he said?* I wondered. *Will he even care? Could he really have a spot for me?*

I decided to write to him. In a confident email, typed with speed and force, propelled by my reaction to being let go from *The View,* I wrote that being Barbara Walters's apprentice for the past ten years had not gone to waste, that interviewing the president of the United States four times was not something that I took lightly, and that with the experience I had, I was ready for whatever challenge was available at FOX. That email had a lot of beef—and a lot of me. It had to. It was basically my resume in short, and time was even shorter.

Barbara had written Mr. Ailes as well, which meant the world to me. She knew me personally and professionally, and frankly, I am not sure a person in our industry could have a more respected referral.

The day came for my meeting with Mr. Ailes.

I arrived at FOX, having prayed all morning long that the meeting would go well. But I was shaking for some reason. It was understandable given that at the time Roger Ailes was the most powerful decision maker in our industry. Judging by the number of doors and checkpoints I was required to go through to get to his office, meeting him personally was no small feat.

"Thank you for meeting with me, Mr. Ailes," I said.

"You can call me Roger," he replied.

"Mr. Ailes," I repeated, insisting on formality. I continued, "I am here for obvious reasons, as I am now ready and have the ability to make a career move to your channel."

Surely he knew from Barbara that ABC had not renewed its contract with me, but I was not yet comfortable enough to say so.

As I was walking by his coffee table, I noticed a five-dollar bill on the floor. I picked it up and handed it to him, saying, "Mr. Ailes, this must be your five-dollar bill." After a quick pause and aiming to break the ice, I added, "I should let you know that I am going to ask for that back in our negotiations."

Quick wit worked.

He smirked. I exhaled.

For an hour, we discussed all the happenings at *The View*, what I would be interested in, in terms of shows, and possibilities.

He expressed several concerns. Was I actually serious about the job? Would I really take an offer? Did I want to wake up early enough to do a morning show? Did I know enough about the Middle East and the political tide? These were all valid concerns.

The answers were all yes.

I told Mr. Ailes, "One thing you need to know about me: my work ethic will exceed my capabilities, but I am always willing to learn, and I love being part of a team."

My new job was unofficially negotiated right there, five-dollar bill and all—with a handshake, a promise, and a "Welcome to the family."

I had gone from hired to fired to hired again. I was back on a team. Another walk-on victory. All it required was waking up at two in the morning and knowing a lot about everything.

What have I truly gotten myself into? I wondered. Zechariah 4:6 came to mind: "'Not by might nor by power, but by my Spirit,' says the LORD Almighty."

Did God provide me with this opportunity? I wondered. *Or did I just go get it and ask Him to bless it?* He allowed it, but was it His will for me? Whether I stole the base or not, the good news (pun intended) was that God met me there, exactly where I was. And being able to work again was blessing enough to stop questioning that.

What I soon realized was that I would be on the best team in morning news—with the most effective research and production minds, a television crew with whom I would trust my life, and cohosts who would lay down their lives for me.

Working with a noncombative team was the most incredible opportunity for me. I went from *The View,* where we talked about relatively easy topics but I felt I was at war, to talking about war while feeling at ease with the team around me. I didn't feel the pressure of thinking they wanted to get rid of me; instead, I pressured myself on the inside because I did not want to let them down. Questions raced through my head: What if they found out that I was not as quick thinking as other people? What if they found out I did not study broadcasting? What if they saw that Middle Eastern foreign policy does not come easily to me or that I was not as talented as they had hoped? What if I was not as quick to ask follow-up questions as they would like? What if I let my team down? What if I didn't have what it takes and they knew it?

New Job, New Schedule, New Challenges

As you might expect, my early wakeup came quickly the day I started at *FOX & Friends.* I had barely shut my eyes the "night" before. I checked my dress and bag several times and then was almost afraid to lie down and fall asleep, fearing I would miss the alarm.

I quickly learned that by the time I arrived at work each day, emails would be awaiting me from our team, who had been up through the night collecting stories and global intelligence updates. Immediately I would read the news bulletin sent to our team, story after story, taking notes and making notes for interviews throughout the course of the three-hour live news program. This was not an opinion program; it was news, and I could not make a mistake. I studied.

Tim and I came up with a plan to make the new schedule work. Two thirty in the morning came with alarm for sure! The last time I was up at that hour, I was either feeding a baby or in college, returning from a night out. All I knew was that I woke up angry and hungry.

Tim was a saint. He woke up with me and made tea, coffee, or blended a green juice. Then he handed me my bag and walked me to the car with an encouraging hug and kiss. Despite my morning mean stage, he loved me, stood by me, and helped me get out the door. Once in the car, a cheery good morning from a driver would start my day.

Reality soon hit as I realized I did not have the stamina I thought I had. I was on the best team of my life, and I was losing on the inside. Yet God met me there. And even though I attempted to do something with my own might, His provision was there. He rescued me from myself, from my will, and from a place where I desperately wanted to be.

Getting up at 2:30 a.m. was not easy for me. It was a privilege to do the job I was doing, especially with the team I was doing it with. So the feeling of *Oh my word, it's 2:30 in the morning* was never without gratitude for the people around me or for the men and women whose stories of bravery we would tell that morning on the air. For me to feel that thankfulness required discipline: I would read *Jesus Calling* while standing on the cold bathroom floor in the dark to get ready. It also required gentleness: a hug from my husband, reassuring me that I could do this.

Picking out an outfit at that time was never easy. At home and in the office, organizing my dresses by color certainly made the morning wardrobe choice easier, as I remembered seeing the other women at FOX doing this very thing. I soon realized that the warmer the dress, the better. Television studios are cold—freezing to be precise—in order to keep the equipment working well and the crew from overheating. The crew actually set up a hidden heating pad for me to rest on and have close by so that I could keep warm! The crew. Can I just take one moment to give them a hug through these pages? There has never been a crew member I did not just love. They are citizens with amazing skills and humility, and they are some of the smartest, most giving men and women I have met.

Back to getting ready in the morning. It wasn't easy but was made easier by the soulful and blessed hearts I have come to know over the years. One of those was Karen Dupiche. God gave me a forever sister in this woman. She is Haitian, gorgeous, funny, smart, loyal as the day is long—and she could make a tired mom who had chips and rice for breakfast look chiseled in five minutes flat! All this *and* she loves Jesus. She was up before I was, and I never heard her complain about getting from her home to the studio by four in the morning. Not once. She could "rise and grind," unafraid of working hard, and make days better for people at the same time. Seeing mornings the way Karen did got me through many an early start. Not only did she have the talent to wave a brush and *conceal* how tired I was as she transformed my face in mere minutes, but she also had the ability to *reveal* God's Word when I needed it most.

Our *FOX & Friends* team began with Steve Doocy and Brian Kilmeade and thrived daily because of the craftsmanship of our technical crew and the amazing brainpower of our production team. It was a team of thoughtful, critically thinking, honest, hardworking patriots who believed that everything we had was a result of the sacrifice made by another brave soul.

Though naturally I am not really an early, early morning person, I am thankful to have spent the mornings during those years with this group. Steve and Brian are forever friends. They answered any question and had my back when it came to tough moments and stressful news days. They understood that I wanted to be with my children, and their families became family to me. They were selfless, caring, and smart, and I just happened to be blessed enough to be greeted by their enthusiasm every morning and to work with them each day.

We had strong leadership, unfailing support, and great people. Being a good teammate was at work all around our offices in Times Square. From the hair and makeup room to the security team to Joel, our stage manager, everyone linked arms each day. Bill Hemmer told me on one of my first days at FOX, "This place is special because everyone has an oar in the water." It was an honor to have my oar in the water with this group.

The challenge of the show was not solely the alarm calling me out of bed in the early morning. Part of the challenge was the trouble I had with calling it a night. This routine certainly taught me about what hours of the day I best function.

"You've got to give up on the day," Tim said each night about eleven as I sat propped up in bed with a snack, my trusty iPad, and notes for an interview. At that late hour, I was often aiming to color-code questions, follow-ups, and research and cram as much information as possible into my brain before the alarm woke me just three and a half hours later.

"I just need two more minutes" was always my response. Haunted by the feelings that I was behind, did not know enough, would not remember enough, had not thought questions through enough, had not highlighted enough—two more minutes regularly turned into two more hours.

It was not as if I felt as though I was running behind because I was lazy or had procrastinated. Any working mom knows it is really hard to get your own items checked off when you desperately want quality time with the kids after school and practices while also making dinner, cleaning up, and overseeing bath time and prayers. Then there was always the list for the next day. I was running in all directions at top speed.

So there I was trying to do what I never felt capable of—cohosting a morning news station during a year with some heavy-hitting moments. Syria, attacks, missing planes, beheadings, and more. I was desperate to get facts right, and my heart sank as I read the realities of the atrocities taking place globally. Even though I was with a great team and in a great career spot and had a great family and a husband who would go to the ends of the earth for me, I felt lost in it all.

I lost sleep. I lost energy. I lost weight. I lost the mornings with my kids. I lost my grip on what was going on with homework, teachers, and friends. I lost the energy to play with the kids when I got home from work. Then I lost the desire to play or have fun—and that is when things got scary. I also lost my sense of taste. Nothing really tasted good, not in my mouth and not in life.

I lost track of dinner items to get for the week. Then I lost the desire to cook. I lost my patience too often and lost the ability to have plain old-fashioned fun without falling asleep on our dinner guests when we had friends over on a Friday.

I lost the feeling of joy in nearly everything I treasured.

I remembered TobyMac's song "Lose My Soul," in which he wrote about not wanting to gain the world yet lose his soul, and I felt assured that if something did not change, this was a possibility—not in faith but in my zest for the everyday part of my life at home.

My time at FOX was one of the best things that ever happened to me. My failure to practice the consistent discipline of sleep in order to match the demands of the job ultimately prevented me from harvesting the fruits of my labor. I was chasing *being capable* and not resting fully in *being called,* and that led me to a mentality of overworking and not surrendering as much as I could have. I was not good at giving up on the day and getting rest. I did not know how and thought I could somehow work my way through the point of exhaustion.

Being a working mom, both then and now, is something I am happy to be.

But during those years at FOX, it was not hard because I was a working mom. The issue was that most days, I was striving at work and barely surviving at home. The areas of life in which I once found joy were leaving me feeling numb.

Interrupted

I was planning to keep pushing through. That is what a good teammate did. That is what I was good at—trying hard, not giving up, not giving in, earning the spot even after I had it. However, in an attempt to overcompensate for how underqualified I thought I was, I fell into striving and failed at thriving.

I spent Monday through Friday expending anything I had in my tank at work because I wanted to do well by my team. I convinced myself that I could keep up the pace. Sadly, I was keeping the pace, yet losing the race. Our great God knew me well enough to bring my fast running to a screeching halt.

A routine checkup became anything but routine when I heard my name begin a sentence with a formal tone. "Mrs. Hasselbeck," the doctor said, "we found a tumor. It is concerning, so we should look at a calendar."

"For what?" I asked.

"Surgery. This needs to be removed immediately, so we can determine what the next step will be . . ."

My mind went blank.

"Mrs. Hasselbeck, how do the next couple of weeks look for you?" asked the doctor. "Mrs. Hasselbeck?"

I was far too exhausted at that point to feel anything, really, so almost without emotion I said, "I don't have time for surgery, Doctor. I have to be at work, and I have three kids who need me."

"Mrs. Hasselbeck," the doctor said, "you don't have time *not* to have surgery. I am recommending that we schedule a procedure in the next month, and I will let you call your husband to discuss the timing."

When you are at Memorial Sloan Kettering Cancer Center seeing the best of the best doctors, you follow the instruction. I could sense concern.

God gave me a break in the form of a medical scare, and sadly it took the necessary anesthesia to allow me more than four hours of real sleep. I slept so long after my procedure that the surgeon had to come in and hit my leg to wake me up after I had been out for more than ten hours!

During the week after surgery, God permitted uncertainty. That, coupled with pain and my tendency to overthink or worry, was a recipe for some really awful days of thinking the worst. The results would take a week. Yet, in the midst of pain and wondering, I parked right in the spot of Scripture. I camped out in sleep.

During that week, I had some of the best days at home I had experienced in more than a year. I knew the biopsy of the tumor was out of my control, and I felt free to pray for a clean bill of health, knowing I would be held by the Maker of the mountains and the Father who knew every hair on my head. There I was—either a mom healing to get ready for "next steps" or a mom who would get a benign report and begin healing to train to run again. An indescribable peace washed over me where I would normally have bathed in worry. The gift of knowing that the unchanging God had gone before me either way calmed me.

In my heart were a joy and a peace that made no sense given the lack of concrete medical information about the tumor. I could never have conjured up such a sense of peace and joy, but it was real, and for me to realize I could feel those two things again took being stuck in bed.

Those days of rest were a coming up for air that I needed. Perhaps that was a signal to change things up again, I concluded. So I decided that once I got back to work, I would try to do just that.

Roger Ailes called to check on me each day I was home. Tim was on his speed dial it seemed. I was thankful he cared.

Resting up brought the joy of playing games with the kids again. We did crafts and painted and sang and baked. The post-op time was like a vacation!

On day eight when I called to get the test results, I was prepared in peace to receive the direction God would give me: benign. Praising God with the peace of whatever that word was going to be was His gift to me.

A Gift That Allowed Me to Get Back on Track

When I was strong enough to get back to work—a little earlier than I should have, but I felt guilty about being out so long—I found a rolling bag to wheel to work in place of my trusty overloaded and oversized tote

(I do not travel light), so I could maneuver my way around the office and in and out of the car without popping my stitches or compromising healing. Once I felt strong enough to get back at it when it came to work, it was not long before my old habits began to sneak in. Slowly, nine hours of sleep became six hours, which became four, then three. And all the crankiness and spikiness returned once I arrived home each day.

I began to hear again the voice that told me I was underqualified—that I had to catch up, that I had missed so much, that I had to prove that I did not miss a beat, that I was not a weak link at *FOX & Friends*. Before long, the walk-on was at it again. And the old pattern snuck its way back into my days because I let it.

I recall the look of concern on the face of my best friend, my soul mate, Tim. He could see what was no longer visible to me: I had lost perspective on a healthy work habit. He knew that I was not running behind; I was running on empty.

God knew me well and allowed a really hard day to show me that a hard decision had to be made. If after the surgery I had returned to my old habits that led to exhaustion, which I believe was His way of trying to get my attention, He would have to allow something tougher to break me. And He did. I had a "terrible, horrible, no good, very bad day." The typical backlash that I had endured for over a decade and a half after commenting on any given news story felt hotter, and I was not as flame resistant as I had felt in the past. Perhaps when you have deprived yourself of sleep, pushed yourself to the limits of performance, and reached a stress level already at a high, anything would sting or burn more. This day in particular was the one that brought me to my knees and showed me that I was, in fact, not enough, and that I was not leaving enough room for the Holy Spirit in my life. It was a day that indicated sharply that it was time for something to change. I had hit a breaking point.

Permission Granted

As Psalm 120:1 says, "I cried to the LORD, and He heard me" (NKJV). God gave me permission to do what I would never have given myself permission to do. He gave me the permission to walk away from my job and leave something that was great—just not great for me at the time. There is a big difference, and I had just learned that the hard way. The lessons I learned about leaving well at *The View* would be applied as I left FOX. This time, however, I was not leaving because I *had* to but because I needed to.

My last day at FOX was unforgettable because I loved the group I was saying goodbye to. It was also unforgettable because, although I had spent the last three years attempting to prove otherwise, I was now actually admitting that I could not do it all as well as I was trying to. *It was time for my family to get the best of me, not the rest of me.* The freedom that came with that realization, for me, was astonishing. I am forever thankful to have been brought to a point where I had to give it all to God. In this case, that required giving up on what I had been holding all on my own.

8

Paper-Bag Lessons

❧

Draw the light, and you will draw the bag.

—Sister Diane

L ife teaches us along the way. Part of what I learned at a young age from a great art teacher has worked its way back into my life. Through her I learned that when painting, it always helps to take a step back and look at the work from a new distance. Likewise, stepping back from broadcasting and news and debates gave me that step-back perspective. Creating space between the impactful moments in my life and the speed at which I was moving through them allowed me to recall one important way to see with a fresh point of view. I invite you into the story of one teacher who opened my eyes and how she allowed me to look back and see the best in all situations.

Sister Diane was one of the most instructive educators I have ever had. One day in my high school advanced art class, she placed a crumpled brown-paper lunch bag on the still-life table, adjusted a spotlight to hit the bag exactly as she wanted, and told us to begin our study of the lunch bag. I sat kneading my gummy eraser, softening it between my thumb and forefinger, unable to begin as my eyes settled on one wrinkle on its surface, then another.

Noticing my state of sketch paralysis, she instructed firmly, "I said, 'Begin.'"

Gulping and kneading my eraser some more, I raised my hand. As she drew near and leaned down, I asked her how it would ever be possible to draw or illustrate all the cracks, crinkles, and folds in that mess of a bag. She simply responded, "I am not asking you to focus on all the dents and cracks and darkness, as they will overwhelm you. I am *asking* you to see the light. Draw the light, and you will draw the bag."

Sister Diane was a proficient art teacher, and looking back at that day, I see now that she was teaching me about more than just a paper bag. Her instruction provided a method to adjust perspective on the challenges of life and a lesson in how to illustrate them. The paper-bag lesson has helped me as I reflect on my tenure at *The View* and my time at FOX News. During that decade and a half, there were certainly dark days, some of which unfolded in front of millions of viewers, while others stole my joy privately and were seen only by God. Some days, like the paper bag, showed cracks, crinkles, and folds during my time there, but there was always plenty of light. And the light, thanks to Sister Diane's teachable moment, is what I choose to focus on; the lessons are what I have chosen to take with me. The value of what I learned at *The View* far outweighs the stress of being outnumbered at the table. The value of what I learned while working on the team at FOX far outshines the hour at which I had to wake up and the depth of the news content.

I'd like to share some of my paper-bag lessons—learned the hard way—with you. With a fresh look at the past set of years that were not in my playbook, I can see how God used all the minutes to bring me closer to Him. I feel comfortable sharing them as I see them now. Some of these are lessons, some are approaches to how I now look at those stumbling blocks, and some are simple illustrations of how the positive light on a subject always brings out the best picture.

Lesson 1: Be Prepared

At *The View*, I had a ten-year apprenticeship with an icon in the broadcasting and television business. It was a decade of being with, learning

from, and studying the best of the best. Working for and with Barbara
Walters remains one of the most educational times of my life. When I
arrived at *The View,* I was newly married, in my midtwenties, and really
inexperienced when it came to television, politics, and debating. By the
time I walked out of the building on that last day, I had three children
and, thanks to her, a wealth of experience.

Whether Barbara planned to interview a child, a prisoner, or a president of the United States, she approached the interview with intentional
preparation. Her notes were lengthy, rewritten, and underlined. If an in-
terviewee had written a book, she would have read and highlighted the
entire book and all its reviews. If the person commented on a chapter, she
could recall it and ask a follow-up question.

When the day came for a guest to arrive on the show, Barbara would
spend the morning sifting through questions, not only her own, refining
along the way the questions of the entire interview. She would then spend
some time with the guest socially to welcome him or her while also making absolutely certain there was not a detail missed—such as something
new to mention or an emotion to share about a hot topic of the day.

Barbara respected the people she interviewed, and she respected
their stories enough not to wing it. Guests felt honored by her preparation and interest. They saw her with their books, tabbed and marked
with written notes. At *The View,* we joked that by the time Barbara
greeted our guests, she would know more about them than they knew
about themselves!

The media has jabbed at Barbara for making people cry. The truth is,
it was not that she made them cry. It was that she was the one person who
read their entire history with interest, listened intently to what they were
saying, and could hear not only their words but their hearts. She could be
fully present in an interview and let people feel safe enough to tell their

stories and share their feelings because she had earned their respect with her vigorous, thorough preparation.

Barbara prepared to listen in the moment, and listen well she did. She is one of the most prepared listeners I know, and she was able to ask brave questions because of that. To this day, I mark a book, as my teacher taught me, and realize that good questions come from being prepared and from being a good listener. She exemplified that for me, and I am forever grateful.

I learned from Barbara the value of having information for the situation. It still humbles me to think that every fifteen minutes I was able to speak life and truth to more than one million viewers. Whether we were talking about marriage, politics, or snacks, I could handle the logistics because I had the statistics.

The lesson I learned is this: prepare to the best of my ability in any situation. Preparation allows room for observation and real listening. Being as prepared as I could be allowed me to appreciate the moments that came in between, be fully present, and have eyes in the moment that allowed me to seek the best in each situation.

Lesson 2: Be Prepared to Be Unprepared

There are some things that you cannot prepare for. Therefore, you must prepare your heart and your mind to be ready for things to change unexpectedly, not go your way, or leave you feeling unprepared. These are the times that call for preparation of the heart to be ready for what you are not ready for. You've got to be prepared to be unprepared—prepared to do the next best thing you can.

Preparing for interviews was part of my work. Preparing to interview presidents was altogether a different animal. A good experience resulted only when I prepared to be unprepared.

President Barak Obama was coming to *The View*. I had interviewed him as a candidate, but now in his role as president of the United States, it was different. It came with a different pressure, as well as a different, exponentially increased level of expectations. That day, Secret Service agents lined the streets around ABC and a security sweep of the studios was underway. The producers' stress levels and adrenaline rushes were high. Our political producer, Audrey, one of the best in the business, asked me for the questions I planned to ask the president. "I am not going to incriminate you with what I am going to ask," I responded with a smile.

I did not want to show my cards, and if I was going to take any backlash from what I was going to ask, I wanted to protect my team.

"Please let the press secretary and the president's team know that I have prepared my interview questions and will ask one about the economy and one about social media and parenting two girls. I don't want you to be responsible for the questions, so I will keep the details to myself."

My parents came to watch, and they were excited about the chance to meet the president and the first lady. They understood what an honor it was for me to be able to personally ask the president a question. The pressure was on. And I had been up the night before writing and rewriting my notes with my trusty Sharpie and a highlighter. After airing the first show live, we were scheduled for a two-hour break before taping the second show with President Obama to be aired the following day.

To ease my stress, I decided to go for a run in Central Park between shows. The pressure was mounting and the lone conservative voice— me—had to be ready and remain calm enough to grasp the brief moment when I could ask my first question without getting interrupted. I prayed to honor the president but to ask a real question. Despite our political differences, I had great respect for the office of commander in chief and wanted to have a thoughtful conversation.

After the first show, everyone heard, "Clear your offices. Security is coming through," as the dogs and security team began the sweep.

We could return in about an hour, they said, to prepare for the next show. Before leaving my office, I glanced at my desk and saw the blue cards ready to go. *Just in case,* I thought, *I will take them with me on the run. Just in case.*

My mom's "better safe than sorry" words came to mind. I had a gut feeling that anything could happen, so I placed them in a plastic bag and hit the six-mile loop in Central Park. My parents and I planned to meet an hour later when we would walk back to the studio where I would shower, get ready for the show, and introduce them to the president.

The run was great, and I giggled about having my notes with me. I prayed and thought and prayed. The plastic bag was sweaty in my hand, and I was thankful that it kept the notes protected. My mom and dad— the most dependable people in the world—were exactly where they were supposed to be an hour later. As planned, we walked back to ABC. Then security stopped us, saying, "The Secret Service is doing another round of sweeps. It will be some time before you can go in."

We waited two more hours in the lobby of ABC. I was hungry; I was tired; I was having that postrun chill that happens when you are in your own sweat long after your body cools down. Finally, when they opened the metal detectors for us to go in, I knew I would have to shower really fast. I was thankful I had my notes.

My mom and dad sent me off with a hug and a prayer, and I ran to my office. "Ten minutes to get ready and get upstairs!" a stage manager yelled. "Ten minutes!"

Ten minutes, I thought, *to shower and get dressed for an interview with the president of the United States? Ten minutes?*

I was panicked, but not fully panicked. Why? Because I was prepared to be unprepared. I had my notes just in case. I had with me the most important item for the task at hand. So, I pulled a dress over a sports top and brushed my hair and within seven minutes, headed upstairs for the show. We made a quick stop for a photo that I knew would mean the world to my mom and dad, who knew how special it was for a citizen to get the chance to shake the hand of a president.

I still had my questions: "Mr. President, how can you say Governor Romney would be bad for the economy, when by the numbers today, your administration *has* been bad for the economy?"

My second question was, "Our nation sees you as the First Father with teenage daughters dealing with social media. They want to follow your lead on this. What boundaries and rules have you set up for them, and what is your advice?"

The president answered both questions with thoughtfulness and ease. He heard them, and I felt honored to have an opportunity to ask questions directly to the president of the United States. In every picture I have seen from that day, no one can tell that I jumped from running clothes into my dress. I had success without the stress because I was prepared to be unprepared. Sometimes, particularly in the big things, life does not go as you originally mapped it out. I've learned you have to be nimble and do the best with what you have. Be ready to do the next best thing, and then you will be able to tell the story about the goodness that came from it (the light on the bag), not just the crinkles along the way.

Lesson 3: Know Your Audience

There were many days when standing firmly on my faith and principles came without one set of hands clapping for my words as I spoke them. Another cohost could recite the alphabet and hear the audience erupt with applause. But if I said "pro-life," everyone was silent. On occasion one brave soul would quietly clap and wave to me during a break, wanting to say "hi" and whisper, "I'm on your side."

"Why are we whispering?" I would whisper back.

"I'm afraid!" was the answer.

The solidarity was replaced with concern some days as I was swimming up the opinion stream against the current like a conservative trout!

During my very first week, after a heated discussion of hot topics, I checked my email. It was not pretty. For every one kind email, hundreds of nasty ones poured in. When I finished reading them, I could not recall what the one encouraging one said, but I was stamped with the hurtful words of the others.

All it took for Joy Behar was seeing the look on my face to know what had happened. "You read the emails, didn't you?" she asked.

"Don't read them. Just don't," she continued.

It was wise advice from someone who had been there. She could sense that I was not going to be able to withstand the hot topics debate in the makeup room, the on-air hot topics, and the emails that would daily fill my inbox. She was right.

Author Ann Voskamp got it right when decades ago she focused on writing for an audience of one—not for herself, for God. It became so clear to me that if I was going to do this job, there would always be an amplified audience of approval or disapproval. On top of that, the "audience of me" was so hard on myself that I would not be able to get me through. I made a decision—I would order my steps according to the knowledge that my audience was God. As a result, I stopped checking email and, for the most part, blocked out groans in the audience or from my cohosts. Even the promise of praise from one side of the aisle had the power to take my eyes off whom I was trying to please at the end of each day. This discipline of focusing on the light on the bag was not easy. I had to purposefully choose to see the light and not let the darkness in comments overtake my heart.

I prayed, "Let the words of my mouth and the meditation of my heart be acceptable in Your sight, O LORD, my strength and my Redeemer" (Psalm 19:14, NKJV). Some days they were, and some days they fell short, but my goal was set: Honor God with everything I could. Knowing my audience, as Ann Voskamp did, got me through the decade at *The View* and will be my guide for the decades to come.

Lesson 4: Whoopi's House

I love Whoopi Goldberg. That shocks many people. Apparently, people are not supposed to love someone who thinks differently than they do. I guess we are not even supposed to like her.

But I don't just *like* Whoopi; I *love* her. In fact, I love her a lot. And my husband, Tim, and our kids love her too—so much so that each year at Christmastime we get together to open the ornament she sends and talk about how much we love her!

She and I started off our friendship on the wrong foot. We approached each other like two stranger dogs at the park—circling, then a little biting, and then . . . forever friends.

What began as enemy status by the world's standards became a life-long friendship because what Whoopi and I know is that life is about people, not politics. When I took my kids to work, they would love on Whoopi, and she would love on them.

I loved how Whoopi was kind to everyone. There is a concern for others about her that I adore and still cherish. She was strong in her positions but did not expect me to change mine. Whoopi has a heart for many. She is a caretaker; she gives the best hugs; she has a welcoming heart that, like our great God, sees people where they are, loves them where they are, and does not leave them there.

Whoopi and I each think the other one is downright crazy when it comes to our stance on any given issue. *We don't think the same, but we love the same*—and that is the key element of our friendship. She calls me "baby," and I call her "Whoop." And we love each other for who the other is instead of hating each other for what we each stand for.

Whoopi's home is one of welcome. Twice a year, she has a big party at her house. I remember her inviting me, along with everyone from our crew, staff, and team. No one was left out. That day, I had the kids at home, and Tim was traveling for work. I hadn't showered, was breastfeeding, and was a plain old momma mess. I called Whoopi to tell her I did not think I could get the kids dressed fancy and ready or get myself a shower to make it to the party on time. I said that we would be late and that maybe I should just stay home. She said, "Baby, come as you are with the people you love. Get something to eat and make yourself at home. I've saved a place for you."

Isn't that heavenly? Really. That is Whoopi.

Come as you are with the people you love.

Grab something to eat and make yourself at home.

I've saved a place for you.

This is what God says to us: "Come. As you are. I have saved a place for you."

Drawing the light when thinking about the people in your life allows you to see how God shines through each of them. Look for the light shining through rather than the crinkles and cracks we all have. After all, we are defined by God's light and His character. Make it a point to spotlight that in all the people in your life.

Whoopi's "sister act" is no act; I count her as my sister on this earth and in heaven!

Lesson 5: Being Right About Something Is Less Important Than Being Right With Someone

Over the course of a fifteen-year career in broadcasting, the muscle of preparing an argument or a perspective on a topic was what refined my argumentative skill—a reflexive and reactive muscle that needed a lot of workouts to maintain the ten-year debate that I had found myself in at *The View*. I could call myself, and have called myself, a recovering right-aholic.

I needed and loved and thrived on being right for a very long time. In my personal life, training to be right started early—right answers on tests, right study habits, right decisions after school, right course selection to get into the right college to have the right path. I even played right field. That's how much I wanted to be right. Professionally, I spent a decade and a half needing to be really right Monday through Friday each week on live television. Being right was what I was trained to do and what I needed to do. But all that emphasis on being right came with a cost—because people have value. We can be very right on an issue and very wrong with a person. Bob Goff has been an awesome teacher on this subject through his book *Everybody, Always*.

When we hold on to being right, it looks like two cars on a single-lane road, face to face and in gridlock. Whoopi Goldberg and I started this way at *The View*. In fact, I'm pretty sure that our first few words to each only had four letters in them. But at some point, we decided that being right with each other would require being a little more wrong. Wrong enough to give someone the right of way.

When we did that and backed up the cars, we experienced the joy and freedom of not having to think the same way while still being able to love the same way. And we decided that being right about an issue was less important than being right with one another because you can be very right and very alone.

I am pretty sure that we are not going to enter into the gates of heaven with God greeting us saying, "Child, I am so proud of you. Look at how right you were." I am more confident that God desires for us to experience the joy of being right *with* one another, not more right *than* another, and that He is asking for where we stand on issues to be way less important and sacred than the God we stand under together. In his book *Befriend*, Scott Sauls wrote, "If I feel more of a kindred solidarity with those who share my politics but not my faith than I feel with those who share my faith but not my politics, what does it say about me?" I think for years I needed to hear this and wish I had.

Think about that person you are less right with because you have been so right about a position, an issue, or something else that matters a lot less than another human being. Being right does not guarantee that we feel joy. I think we can all be honest and say that we wish we had been a little more wrong—wrong enough to make things right with a sister, a brother, a friend, a husband, a daughter, or a son. What would it look like to be less right about whatever the issue was and be more right with the other person? Bob Goff has taught me a lot about this just by how he lives. Find a teacher who points you to being right with people. Then implement the strategy. Over the past decade, I have learned that working hard at making the point has proven way less fulfilling than pointing to the Maker.

Lesson 6: Treasure Your Trenchips

"Trenchips" are friendships found in the foxholes of life, when friends stand together in tough situations and have each other's backs against enemy fire. Veterans have something the rest of us get a taste of once in a while: they know what it is like to count on and be counted on. We can learn a lot from their devotion to their brothers and sisters in uniform.

Maria Goff wrote in her book *Love Lives Here,* "Sometimes when we're asking Him for an answer, He sends a friend." I sure needed answers at many points in my life, and He sure did send me a friend.

When all was new and uncertain for me at *The View,* Meredith Vieira was this kind of friend to me. She comforted me and exemplified what having kids and a job in our industry could look like. She brought cookies and was caring toward me, and she and I shared lots of hugs during tough times.

Sherri Shepherd was also this kind of friend to me at *The View,* as were many of the producers and crew members who gave me a wink or a smile in a time of trial.

Sherri was there on the hardest of days, and I know that was by God's design. At times, she would come into my office barefoot with heels in hand, drop her fantastic shoes, and say, "Girl, let's pray." That kind of fellowship got me through many difficult days. It takes faith to stand firm and a friend in faith to hold that mast. Sherri held my hand. Sherri taught me how to be a trench mate. She and I sometimes took our children, Jeffrey and Grace (born just weeks apart), to work and let them run the hallways of *The View*. Because she was willing to be bold and to pray with me and for me, Sherri was a bright light in my life on the darkest of days.

Kathie Lee Gifford stood in the trenches with me at a time when the Upper West Side of New York City looked like a politically one-sided minefield for me. It was a place where on Election Day, both my husband and I received a strange pause when we asked for a Republican primary ballot. "Oh . . . we might have one of those . . ." was the reply. It was assumed that everyone leaned left politically, and when you didn't, sometimes there was a social price to pay. For me, it was always going to be worth the price to be open about my faith, not wavering on the right to life for the unborn, particularly for children with Down syndrome, and expressing my heart on faith issues, along with supporting our military men and women and our veterans. It meant that a very public, on-air split-screen battle in which I would not waver in defending the character of those who defended our freedom was worth it. But I felt lonely in the city at times, and many people took a step back from me. Kathie Lee leaned in and is a true trench mate.

My teammates at FOX as we braved the morning hours—knowing our task of bringing the news of those who fight for our freedom was just a slice of the challenges they were willing to face—were my trench mates, together bringing the stories of the brave to the homes of the free. When times feel dark and I need to be refocused on the Word of God, on the good, and on the positive, I am thankful for these friends who—like Sister Diane—popped the spotlight on the bag that felt overwhelmingly full of shadows.

During a time when the world was full of heavy news that I was delivering, Jeannie Cunnion was that kind of friend to me. I wrote in the foreword of her book *Mom Set Free:*

> She is the girl who—when I am soaked in worry or shame or
> hurt or sadness or stress, or when I am being ridiculously hard
> on myself—redirects my eyes to the truth of Jesus, which sets
> my heart free again.

I have witnessed trenchips form around moms battling their cancer or whose kids have walked through cancer treatment. I have seen dads rally around a friend who lost a job or lost a child.

I am joyfully in the trenches with women every day, aiming to raise our kids right and care for our families, lift their hearts, and hold careers. Friends, I pray we are drenched in trenchips with one another. My Nashville moms and friends, I am so honored to be in trenchip with you—to know that we have each other and we lift one another up. Trenchips happen when we do life together, when we walk with one another, when we sling big things together. To all the women who have been in the trenches with other women: Keep at it, keep on being there, cheering one another on.

When things get scary or tough or hard, who has been there for you? When life has gotten scary and hard for someone you care about, have you gotten in the trenches with that person? I have a feeling—and first-hand experience—that is exactly where friendship is found.

Lesson 7: Read the Good News
Before the Hard News

As I mentioned in the last chapter, getting up for those 2:30 a.m. mornings while working for FOX was rough. But the one thing that made such a difference was filling up first on the Word and promises of God before anything else. Scripture puts everything else in its place. Tim's dad exemplified this for me. He spent mornings in quiet time, and I witnessed how being busy or even having to get up early was no excuse for not spending time in the Word. Who gets the first minutes of your heart each day? Who gets the last? These questions are important.

When my alarm went off, the newsfeed was yelling for my attention. But I needed the good news before the hard news. This allowed me to hear what God was saying to me personally through the day and afforded me the blessing of keeping the good news as the first news.

Before I even turned on my light on those early mornings, I crawled across the room with my glasses, my eyes to my phone, so I could read *Jesus Calling* by Sarah Young (I learned that having my Bible and that devotional both in hard copy on the floor and electronically on my phone worked best for me). Those readings are what I balanced the rest of my day against, and I needed a multifaceted way to make sure I could access the truth all day long.

Videographers and photographers often achieve what is called white balance by holding a sheet of white paper or cardboard in front of the camera to get a look at the true white. Then all the other colors are balanced against it.

My morning devotional and Bible reading was my white balance. Not just in case I needed it, but because I would definitely need it. I would need and want to see everything else's color in the light of that Word. God's Word is the light against which all else is weighed. The knowledge that some hard news was going to penetrate my mind and heart early and often, as the job required, created a need and discipline for me to fill up on the good news first. This habit, though I'm not in broadcasting anymore, is one I hope never to break.

Lesson 8: Be a Daily Patriot

At FOX, I was wonderfully overwhelmed by how each and every day we had the chance to honor the United States military. Talk about seeing the best of our nation, the bright part of the nation first! I can remember feeling blessed to shine light on those who are willing to protect our freedoms each day. I am forever thankful that I could allow everyone at home a chance to pause for those who ask for no applause.

"Freedom ain't free." "We are free because they are brave." Those are not just expressions; they are actuality. The very opinions we have the right to hold are protected by those willing to lay down their lives for this right and others. As Jesus says in John 15:12–13, "My command is this: Love each other as I have loved you. Greater love has no one than this: to lay down one's life for one's friends."

Their families make sacrifices, and when those in the military return from serving our nation, it is our turn. Being a member of Team Red, White, and Blue (www.teamrwb.org)—which connects veterans to their communities through physical and social activity—and being at FOX have helped me feel close to these people. Understanding that this nation is bright because of the brave is crucial for me. Our nation *is* truly great, but it has trouble and pain and wrongdoing and all the things that come

with a fallen world. Gratitude for the freedom in our nation and ultimately the freedom of the Cross is my choice of perspective. It means that
my heart goal each day is one of citizenship and honor and thanksgiving
for the price that is, and was, paid for those freedoms.

Lesson 9: Pay Attention to the American Stories

Hearing the stories every day on *FOX & Friends* of Americans doing
great things made me a better citizen. It's so important to listen to their
stories and pass them on. I still have a letter from a World War II veteran
whom I had the chance to interview and learn from as I listened to his
wisdom. Making wooden toys for children, he sought purpose each day.
One piece of wood at a time. Knowing his story and passing it on to my
children is a joy.

Share the stories of our nation's heroes. Shine the light on them.

Lesson 10: It Is Possible to Learn Something New
at Any Age, So Do That as Often as Possible

For me, learning to deliver hard straight news after ten years of having to
give a hard opinion first was not easy, but it was not impossible. Learning
something new is an incredible time for growth. But give yourself time to
settle in. From my experience, feeling settled at work or in a new job or in
a new set of skill demands takes about a full year and a lot of patience.
Sometimes learning demands all your patience. But mark your progress!
The light on the bag shows through the steps you are taking. Ask God to
move your heart toward the learning. It will shape you, but it just takes
time!

Lesson 11: Teamwork Matters

Having been on a lot of teams, I can say that FOX was one of the best, as it provided me with a work environment that valued honesty, loyalty, and wanting others around you to do well. I asked a lot of questions and felt able to do so because everyone wanted others to do well. No one was too prideful to help or ask. Humility and sacrifice for the whole was real in that office.

Many of our mornings with friends included jerseys or team uniforms for obstacle courses or challenges. I am proud to have worn a jersey for this team. Being optimistic and encouraging matters. Don't be the teammate who calls out every lump and bump on the way up the mountain as reason to stop. Instead be the teammate who comments on the view you have from the top once you get there and encourages steps along the way.

Lesson 12: Find a Mentor and Be a Mentor

I asked a lot of questions before I started the job at FOX and sought wisdom from those who had been there long before me. Once you have experienced something, be willing, ready, and joyful when it comes to sharing your experience with someone stepping into what you have walked through. Asking questions does not make you weak, and you are never too busy to offer your ear and wisdom to someone else when asked. Do both as often as you can: ask for someone to light the path for you, and do not hesitate to shine it before someone else's feet as they begin their steps. Have you ever had someone with a flashlight light the path in front of you as you walked back from the beach or the backyard in the darkness? Your steps immediately become assured, your heart is immeasurably thankful, and you get to the next point with ease. Light the path ahead for the next person.

Lesson 13: "Give Up on the Day Before It Gives Up on You"

My best friend, love of my life, and the hardest-working man I know, my husband, Tim, spoke these words to me: "Give up on the day before it gives up on you." He values rest. He is wise to do it. In the years when I took rest for granted, although it is something that God designed us for, things did not go well. I learned the hard way that lack of sleep is not good for me and is not good for those around me. Don't wait until your children say things like: "Mommy, remember when you used to put your head down and fall asleep on the kitchen table all the time?" and "Remember when we would have to wake you up and then you would cry?"

When your four-year-old draws a picture of you and then gets closer and reaches for a red marker to "add one more thing" (the red veins in your eyes), it is time to rest. Give yourself the permission to turn the light off. Because if you don't sleep, everything looks dark—even in the daylight.

Lesson 14: Moms Are All Full-Time Moms

Those who are moms, whether we are working moms or stay-at-home moms, we are all full-time moms and we are on the same team. We need each other. Every pitcher needs a catcher. Let's be there and lift each other up. Encourage one another and see the how the light hits and shines on and through each woman in your life.

Lesson 15: Connections Matter

Barbara Walters's support had a huge impact on my getting the job with FOX. Tim's dad got me my first internship and apprenticeship, which led to my getting a job. I would never have gotten the job at Puma without that connection. It would have been easy for me to feel less than welcome or able because someone else did it for me. I decided to be not prideful but thankful—and to serve the workplace I was in as if a gift had been given to me. Nothing truly is ours anyway through our own efforts. Remembering that it is all from God makes it something to appreciate, not spite, when connections happen. Seeing the connections as a means of actualizing gratitude and working hard in thanks gives the work greater purpose.

Lesson 16: Be Your Sister's Keeper

Having a significant impact in our workplace rests largely on being willing to speak up for the woman closest to us and closest to a potentially violating situation. What would it look like if we actually cared more about one another than we care about edging one another out? Women need each other, and we need to be a voice of warning, concern, and help. Connect and protect one another in the moment. Work as hard at being kind as you work at getting the job and keeping the job. Be the kind of teammate you would want your daughter to have. Raise your daughters (and sons) to have a voice for others.

Seeing the light on the paper bag does not mean denying that there are some cracks and crinkles in it. It simply offers a discipline for how we choose to illustrate the challenging times in life. God, I believe, is asking us not only to see the light but also to reflect His light. I find it more effortless to reflect His light when I have practiced noticing, spotting, and choosing to see the light instead of the darkness, and I am so thankful for great teachers and friends who continue to be lights each day for me!

Lesson 17: Really Letting Go Takes Time

Letting something go takes prayer and time. As challenging as it was at times, my position at *The View* was something I would have done anything to keep. My grip was tight. Although I could let go of it in my head, it took about six years for my heart to match what I had been asking it to feel. The checkup on my true sentiments came with a call I never thought I would get: *The View* was asking me back.

Jim Ornstein, my broadcasting agent, let me know that ABC wanted to talk with me about something. Hours later, I was on the phone with an ABC executive who told me they wanted me back in the chair five days a week. *The chair I had? The chair they had truly pulled out from under me? That chair?*

Six years after they took *that chair* away, they were offering it to me again. I would have anticipated my response to be "Nice try, I'm busy now" and hanging up the phone. But God had changed my heart over the years. He allowed me to leave well enough, to heal well enough, and to hear that call as an invitation in my right-now grace instead of my back-then resentment. I decided to pray about the offer and talk to Tim. Making sure I could hear God's direction was more important than anything else. Through prayer, peace about the decision came. And with that, I also felt thankful that they asked me back. Though I could neither picture myself back in that arena nor imagine moving our family out of Nashville—a place God carved out as our home—I could see all that He had done in my heart. He healed the wound of disappointment and betrayal, and He provided me with gratitude. God gave me the freedom to let go of the very thing that I would have done anything to hang on to six years earlier. He released my grip even more.

He gave me the time and space to reflect on that ten-year period of *The View* and really sink into the bright spots on the paper bag!

9

Invited

❧

Darling, you must go.

—Barbara Walters

On what began as a typical weekday morning, I had the unbelievable honor of opening an invitation to a White House state dinner honoring the queen of England on May 7, 2007. It arrived by mail—not email, real mail. I mean, really fancy *real* mail, with a seal on the envelope.

How did I get here? I asked myself. How did this girl not yet thirty years old, from Cranston, Rhode Island, get to this place in New York City, receiving an invitation for a meal with the queen?

And what was a girl to do when she received such a fancy invitation? I took it to the fanciest person I knew at the time, Barbara Walters. When I knocked on her already-open office door, the smell of morning coffee and a light breakfast was almost as welcoming as Barbara herself. "Come in," she said. "Tell me what's on your mind."

There was something I loved about having time with Barbara alone. Sometimes I just popped into her office for no reason but then made up a reason just to be near her. It reminds me of the way one of my young children would call my name to get my attention and then come up with a reason. Barbara was always the first to know what was happening in the news world; she was also the first to know what was happening in my personal world. I knew that whenever I had something to announce or report, I should go to her first—partially out of respect and partially because she made my news seem as important as the latest global issue. When I went to her about the state dinner invitation, what I shared was big news indeed!

After I explained the fancy invite, Barbara told me, "Darling, you must go."

"But, Barbara," I said, "I would have to travel, and I would have to miss Grace's swimming lesson that afternoon, and I have never been away from her. I feel going out of town for one dinner might be too much."

"You must, darling. You *must*," she insisted.

"What do I do?" I asked her. "What do I wear? How do I greet her? Do I curtsy?"

Barbara's smart, practical, certain, wise advice followed my stream of questions, as it usually did.

"Wear gloves and a pretty suit or dress. Nothing too revealing. Cover your shoulders with a jacket, perhaps, in case the room is cold. You are pregnant, so know that you will be standing for quite some time and make sure your shoes can withstand that. Eat before you go, as you want to take care of the baby. Tell Tim to rent a tuxedo. This will be a formal event, so do whatever the queen does first. Do not lift a glass until she lifts one, do not stand until she stands . . ."

When Barbara finished, she emphasized again, "Just do whatever the queen does."

I repeated that advice in my mind for days. *Just do whatever the queen does. Just do whatever the queen does.* Got it.

Tim and I said a tearful goodbye to Grace, as leaving her for the first time felt pretty awful . . . on top of already feeling a little queasy.

When we arrived at the White House, I was surprised to find that the state dinner was a small, intimate affair involving approximately forty guests. Every time we walked into a different room, someone announced us, and it felt like part of the movie *Cinderella* when the girls are announced for the prince. At one point, Tim and I got such a kick out of being announced that we walked in and out of one room twice, just for effect. It was the most exquisite night I have ever been part of.

As we made our way through the White House, a member of the United States military stopped us, addressed us by name, and motioned for us to step closer to him. (*How did he know our names?* I wondered.) We had been found out, I concluded, and were about to be reprimanded for having a little fun with the name announcements.

As we moved toward him, I held my breath and tried to formulate a proper apology for ducking in and out of rooms just for amusement. I was about to pour out the apology when he said, "Ma'am, I just want to thank you for all that you have done."

"All that I have done?" I questioned.

"Yes, ma'am. All that you have done, as you have been vocal about supporting the military and our family members. I need to let you know what that meant."

"Well, that's nothing compared to all that you and your brothers and sisters do for us each day to protect our freedoms. So please, let me thank you instead," I said to the kind, decorated serviceman.

That moment, between rooms, this protector of our freedoms thanked me. The music stopped (at least in our heads). It did not matter whom we were about to say hello to because in that moment, God allowed me to see that words have meaning. I had been challenged vehemently on the hot topics just before I saw him, but all that tension was worth it in that moment with him. That was the first time I had been face to face with someone I had never met who had been affected by something I said. And from that point on, I promised myself that I would continue to be a voice for those who protect the freedom that allows the rest of us to be heard.

Upon arriving to greet the president of the United States, First Lady Laura Bush, Queen Elizabeth, and Prince Philip, my mind went completely blank. I could not remember how to address them properly, so I ended up in something like a bow and a curtsy in front of the queen, and following the formalities, we lined up and a photographer snapped the photo.

Clutching Tim's arm as we made our way through the dining room, I was thankful we had a plan because of my being gluten-free and allergic to almost everything. Our game plan was for him to eat from his plate, then secretly swap it for my full plate so no one would realize I had not eaten. He would then pass me what appeared free of allergens since I was one hungry momma-to-be.

We quickly realized our plan would never work as we were seated at different tables. Apparently, I now joke, the people in charge of seating at fancy dinners separate loved ones! This was terrifying to me because while Tim was relaxing at what we called the kids table, celebrating with chocolates and cheers along with the Bush daughters and recent Kentucky Derby–winning jockey Calvin Borel, I was seated just one table away from the queen. The guests at my table included Prince Charles, Secretary of State Condoleezza Rice, the queen's lady-in-waiting, and Governor Jeb Bush. Lots of medals, lots of official titles, lots of perfect posture.

The entire evening, this gluten-free, pregnant, hungry girl was just waiting for something *not* breaded to eat. More importantly, I kept my eyes on the queen, just as Barbara had told me. The violins playing throughout the room kept anyone from hearing my grumbling stomach, but despite the fact that I really wanted something to eat, many moments during the dinner made me feel as though I were dreaming or had stepped back in time to play a starring role in a movie. At other times, I felt like someone who had ventured too far out into the ocean, as though I didn't belong and didn't know what to do. Surrounded by talk of travel to the Middle East and trade agreements, but no gluten-free pizza in sight, I was almost dizzy.

Fearful of missing another Mother, May I? moment with the queen, I continued to watch her. When she stood, I stood. When she sat, I sat. *So far, so good,* I concluded. I was not going to mess this up—or so I thought.

By what seemed to be the nineteenth course of the meal, with pieces of gold-plated silverware slowly dwindling around my plate, something on the table caught my attention. At the time, I thought it was the prettiest bowl I had ever seen. With shiny gold-etched details, it appeared to contain something gluten-free. It had to be safe for me!

I picked up the bowl as carefully as I could, planning to gulp down the entire serving of rose-infused lemonade or whatever it was. Just as the bowl touched my lips, Governor Bush leaned over to me ever so calmly and said, "You might not want to drink that. *It's for your hands.*" I should note, by the way, that drinking from the finger bowl was not something I had seen the queen do.

Governor Bush leaned in—and that made a big difference. Had he simply ordered in a loud or stern voice, "Don't drink that!" I would have felt isolated or judged, maybe a little foolish, and definitely more out of place.

Instead, he simply gave me the facts and let me decide what to do as he said, "You might not want to do that . . ." He gave me information so I could choose my next step. And believe me: I could not put down that bowl of rose-infused water fast enough!

I am fairly certain the queen witnessed the whole thing.

Leaning In

Do I love to tell the story about dinner with the queen because it is so unthinkable that I was at a dinner with the queen or because it's a lesson in how to avoid drinking hand wash? No. I share it because leaning in is the first of three steps in making a difference—in learning how to work purposefully with other people. By "leaning in" I mean watching or listening, learning, and being willing to get involved for the benefit of someone who needs it. The two other steps, which I will explain later in this chapter, are holding up and slinging big things.

When Governor Bush leaned in and spoke to me, he kept me from making a major social faux pas, but most of the time leaning in is needed and can happen in the ordinary moments of everyday life in common places and situations. Leaning in requires seeing people where they are and being willing to enter their space and their circumstances. Sometimes leaning in looks like simply letting people know that you are with them or that you are praying for them. Sometimes it involves leaving your own comfort zone and stepping into someone else's discomfort.

Leaning in looks like being present and encouraging for the people around us. It means being a part of events and moments that speak life. Leaning in calls for conversation, not condemnation. And it looks a lot like love.

Holding Up

When Moses' hands grew tired, they took a stone and put it under him and he sat on it. Aaron and Hur held his hands up—one on one side, one on the other—so that his hands remained steady till sunset. (Exodus 17:12)

In Exodus 17, the Israelites found themselves in their first battle after leaving their captivity in Egypt, on their way to the Promised Land. Moses prayed over that battle for them and watched it from a nearby hill. He prayed with his hands raised. As long as he kept his hands up, the Israelites—the good guys—were winning.

But Moses's arms grew tired, and he was eventually unable to hold up his hands. When his hands were not raised, the Israelites found themselves overwhelmed by their enemy. The good guys weren't winning anymore. So two of Moses's friends, his brother Aaron and a man named Hur, stood on each side of him and held up his hands until sunset.

What I've learned from this story is that if Moses's arms and hands grew tired, yours and mine will get tired too. Moses was the one who commanded the Red Sea to part. This was the guy who insisted that Pharaoh release God's people. He was the boss! And even his arms grew weary.

We must lean in for one another just as Aaron and Hur did for Moses, holding up the arms of the people around us, drawing on God's strength together. We can hold up the arms of those who cannot hold up their hands alone.

Sometimes you and I will be like Aaron and Hur, and sometimes we will be like Moses. We will be the ones who need to keep our arms raised in certain situations. Imagine how encouraged we would be as we face the challenges and pursue the goals we set for our lives if we could trust that our friends would be there to raise our arms joyfully because they had already leaned in. When our friends hold our arms up, and when we do the same for them, then we can all sling big things. That's the next step in working purposefully with other people.

Slinging Big Things

A couple of years ago, a friend came to visit us. After a fun welcome, he remembered that he had forgotten something and returned to his car to get it. Within minutes, he bounded up the driveway with presents for our three kids to play with. Slingshots. Real ones.

I need to mention that I have two boys who love to break things, so my first thought about this friend's gifts was, *Oh my word. They are going to destroy the house.* My second thought was, *Oh my word. They are going to destroy the house!*

"Watch them!" our friend encouraged me.

I was watching all right. He could be certain that I was watching indeed—just as I had watched the queen at that state dinner years previously. I gave my youngest son the "I am watching you" look when I pointed two fingers at my eyes and then turned them to point toward his. Yet, because I trusted our friend, I decided not to give further instructions but to be quiet and simply observe the kids from afar as the adults talked. The excitement was high, and questions poured in to me:

"Mom! Can I sling the Ping-Pong ball?"

"Sure!" I said.

"Can I sling a marshmallow?"

"Sure."

"Can I sling an Oreo cookie?"

Hmm. I wondered if I could say no with our friend standing right beside me, but I didn't. "Sure," I replied.

"Mom! Can I sling a banana?"

The more items the kids wanted to sling, the bigger the smile on our friend's face grew. It was as though he was seeing and saying, "See? They want to sling bigger and bigger things!"

That was the lesson my friend wanted to teach us—that slinging big things is what people are made to do. When we realize this, we can do some really awesome things together.

This friend has been mightily encouraging to identify the "rocks"— our dreams, our goals, our challenges—and launch them. See, slinging big things requires stretching because what we can accomplish is determined by how far we are willing to stretch personally and how far we are willing to stretch for one another. The good news is that we don't have to do it alone. We have Aarons and Hurs who will hold up our arms.

A Life-Changing Lunch

Sometimes leaning in happens when you are at dinner with the queen, but often it happens when you're with friends. More likely than not, you have felt someone be willing to lean in and share what is on your heart.

The invitation to dinner with the queen was one thing I was so thankful to receive. Ten years later, I was even more thankful to be invited to a birthday lunch for my friend Jamee. We had been introduced while knee deep in salty water on a beach with our babies. Her ease of heart and intentional listening gifts were apparent that day, and her company on a sandy beach provided a dose of comfort at my time of big career transition (between *The View* and FOX). I didn't realize it at the time, but God was then laying the foundation of friendship for when we would move to Nashville as her neighbor. God knew that she would be a dear friend to me, long before I could have ever imagined moving. God knew that her birthday lunch—just like that day on the beach—was about something bigger.

The group of women that gathered joyfully around Jamee on her birthday wanted to reciprocate both the kindness and the ear she lent on a regular basis. Since I was still new to Nashville at that point, I was just happy to witness her lifelong friends gathering for her big day. Sweet and thoughtful hearts caught up on the latest, and real conversations happened in those moments.

One of the moms at the table, named Farrell, whom I had been getting to know, leaned in and we began talking. When I asked her how her week was going, she shared with me that there was a little boy who needed help. Big help. I could see the concern and sense the depth of her heart. As she told me of a family that was trying to rescue this little boy and give him a chance to live, I leaned in more closely. Ferlando was three years old and had only one eye because a tumor, a retinoblastoma, was taking over the other one. In fact, the tumor was stealing not only his vision but would also rob him of his life unless something could be done to help him.

He needed the sophisticated, advanced medical treatment that could only be found in the United States. A couple named Rachel and Aaron saw Ferlando, leaned in, and wanted to rescue him.

I spent the next couple of days thinking about how Ferlando could get to Nashville for treatment, how much he needed help, and how this family saw him with his one eye and were willing to do whatever it took to bring him to a place to find healing. They had seen him exactly where he was, in need of a rescue, and were willing, like a pair of shepherds, to go to Haiti and attempt to bring him to Nashville.

But how? How would he get there? Immediately I reached out to my friend Karris Hudson, who has dedicated her life to raising, caring for, and parenting children at Danita's Children in Ouanaminthe, Haiti. Without hesitation, she leaned in and heard the story—and was able to connect with Rachel and Aaron and their two children.

I remember thinking that this was a really big rock to sling, and I had no idea how to do such a thing. How does one save a boy and get him to a place of healing? How can you stretch the band when you don't even know the direction to sling the very thing you are trying to launch?

Instinctively, I reached out to my friend who brought the slingshots. I explained the desperate situation, the heart of this family—a mom and dad and two kids who wanted to give Ferlando a chance at life.

Do you know what my slingshot friend said?

"Let's go get him!"

I almost dropped the phone. Sure, he was a pilot. He could fly, but that is not what nearly stopped my heart. It was that he was willing to go. Willing to put someone's rescue ahead of his plans and willing to help. He made going to rescue a little boy in Haiti sound easier than Amazon Prime. It was his available heart that nearly stopped mine. He was willing to sling big things for others, and his encouragement gave the entire team an emotional boost because he was willing to become a part of it. Just. Like. That.

I am pretty sure that if God had a touchdown dance, He would have been doing it when this exchange took place, as He witnessed someone willing to lean in and hold people's hands up while they are holding up the arms of someone trying to sling big things.

The friend who brought our family slingshots and taught us that we are made to "sling big things" could have said, "That is just so awful. I'm sorry to hear about it." And left it. But he walked the walk. He was willing to do what many others were not—to lean into that situation, to that little boy's life, and hold up the arms of others who could help.

Sometimes God asks us to lean in, uphold, or sling something big through giving our finances, our hearts, our time, or our energy. Sometimes we have to give up something—such as our fears or our comfort. But His promise is that He is with us, and as we lift and hold each other up while aiming to sling big things, He holds us.

Leaning in and stretching is not always possible. I wanted to go to Haiti to help bring Ferlando to Nashville, but as it turned out, my passport had expired. Rachel and Aaron were able to fly there and to provide a medical rescue and medical visa for him.

Their hearts knock me right out of my chair because they saw him exactly where he was, in Haiti, and as he was, with a tumor growing and only one eye left, and they loved him enough to leave everything and risk everything to bring him where they believed he would have a home and a chance at a new life. They risked exchanging all that they had for what God had for them. And because they were willing to stretch, we all got a glimpse of heaven through this little boy when he arrived in the States.

What this family did echoes what God does for all His children. He sees us exactly as we are and exactly where we are, and He pursues us, stopping at nothing to bring us home to give us life.

Tim, Grace, Taylor, Isaiah, and I got a chance to have sideline tickets for their display of love and affection and devotion to this boy who loved being funny and riding his "machine," which was what he called his rideable four-wheeler toy truck.

On one of the rainiest days that I can recall in Nashville, Farrell and her husband, David Mason, invited us all to gather alongside some families who had been praying and loving on Ferlando with Rachel and Aaron. We made our way up a hill to their home through the pounding rain.

Despite the downpour, we all made it—including my slingshot friend and our friend Karris, who came from Haiti to be near him and join in prayer. This was a day of seeing arms lifted. We sat on the floor in a circle with all our children. We prayed with Ferlando running in the center of the circle smiling and laughing. Ferlando—as if he knew how far one friend in particular had been willing to go for him—ran to him, as my slingshot friend smiled back at him and lifted him up high "like a plane." Ferlando grabbed his big grown-up glasses and held them up against his own small face. Peering through the lenses, he smiled the biggest smile, looking around in wonder with a joy that was unspeakable.

It was apparent to me then and is stamped in my heart how much joy comes with looking at life through the right lens. My friend, who did not just tell me about slinging big things, made doing big things for others seem easy and made leaning in and loving well seem simple. Like Ferlando, we should all look through the lens of people like this. Through the story of a little boy with one eye, we all got to line up behind the lens of love, and everything became pretty clear.

Ferlando has a story with palatable purpose and broad reach. I hope you can hear it from the hands and hearts of Rachel, Aaron, and their children one day. Their humility and sacrificial love for others is illustrated by their selfless, joyful willingness to see, seek, and help a little boy on his way home to heaven. They were willing to take the risk of losing him if it meant loving and honoring him well, here on earth.

Ferlando is now smiling with joy and eyes wide open in the lap of Jesus. Our family came to love him, and so we grieve with many others as we miss him here on earth. Our loss is heaven's gain. Ferlando, the little boy with one eye who needed a rescue and a home, opened our eyes to what God's pursuit and love for all of us looks like, and he will one day welcome all of us home to heaven with those big kisses he shared with us here. I'm just thankful to have witnessed up close, hearts that are willing to lean in, lift, and hold each other's arms up to sling big things.

Invitations come in the mail, and they come in the heart. Some invitations are to a person's party with presents, and others are into their present state of pain. God's invitations to be with people come in both types, even at the same time. He is waiting on our yes.

His most important invitation is to ask Him into your heart. Once the door is unlocked there, the rest of the invitations He brings your way are much clearer.

10

The Right Tool
at the Right Time

You deserve all forty ounces.

—Mom

My mom knows I love peanut butter, almond butter, and pretty much any butter in a jar. In fact, when I got back from the Australian outback after filming *Survivor,* I could often be seen with a jar of peanut butter tucked under my arm and a spoon in my hand. Years later, I'm still eating apples covered with peanut butter, drinking peanut butter smoothies, and making peanut butter sandwiches for the kids and Tim. His favorite lunch is a good old PB and J.

One day, my mom was with me in the kitchen and had a little smile on her face—the kind that told me she knew something fun and was waiting for the moment to share it with me.

She handed me a tiny little spatula and said plainly, "Elisabeth, I watch you scraping and scraping at that jar with the butter knife. And you never are going to get it all that way. The forty ounces of peanut butter are paid for. You love it, and you should have all of it, *but you are using the wrong tool.*"

"Really, Mom?" I asked.

She looked back and matter-of-factly said, "You paid for all of it. You should have all of it."

I could not put that spatula away fast enough, but one day about three years later, I was making a sandwich and, for some reason, decided to give it a try. Sure enough, when I used the tool she gave me, I was able to get all forty ounces of the peanut butter out of the jar! *All* of it.

In the jar of life, God wants us to have all forty ounces too. Every last line and drop. He says to us, "I want you to have all the joy." His Son paid for it this time.

But when we use the wrong tool—for example, the stiff butter knife of pride and not the flexible tool of humility—we leave joy in the jar. God wants us to have not just thirty-eight ounces but the whole forty ounces of joy He has for us, and He has given us the tool of humility to get it by His power.

If being right makes me wrong with the people God has placed in my life, then I pray, "God, make me wrong enough. Make me less right so that I can be right with others."

I am so thankful that God has given us all the tools we need, including the spatula of humility, so we can have the whole forty-ounce jar of joy He has already paid for.

Godversations

Using the spatula of humility would have come in handy when I originally began talking to my *View* cohosts about Jesus. But I was using a rigid tool of pride instead. Thankfully, it is not too late. In early 2018, I had what I call a "Godversation" with Joy Behar for the first time, many years after we began working together!

A Godversation, in my lexicon, is a conversation minus condemnation when talking about God.

I posted this on social media:

A #Godversationhappened. Matthew 18 tells us to go direct. So . . . I called up @joyvbehar. This is how the call started. But

it's not anywhere near being finished. What came after laughter
and a quick catch-up was a conversation without condemnation.
She heard why I "hear God" in prayer, in quiet time, through a
friend's discernment, through the power of the Holy Spirit in
the nudges that I feel each day, in the longings of my heart, in the
questions in my heart. And I heard her questions. And I want to
hear her doubts. I love that we are in a country that was founded
on freedom in faith. When my flesh wanted to react and defend
my God and those that were mocked for believing and hearing
Him, I stopped and listened. I heard God remind me that He is
the Defender that cares for us. He cares for Joy too. For 10 years
she and I debated, and reacting in those situations perhaps I could
have offered a more tender witness to this awesome God—instead
many times I reacted. Did I always show grace . . . sometimes not.
And sometimes I felt the need to stand firm and be bold. For now,
I pray to always be able to have grace-filled #Godversations like
this, and I know for sure God wants us to love one another above
all. Even when we disagree.

It just took the right tool. The tool of conversation, not the tool of
condemnation.

Sometimes It Takes Scissors

I love to run. Running clears my mind; it lets me breathe. I love it so much
that I will often run through pain—oftentimes leading to injury.
  Once after struggling with some significant discomfort in my heel
for a week or so and deciding to take on six miles anyway, I found myself

midrun unable to take another step forward. After calling Tim for a ride home (Did I mention he is also my hero?), I realized the odd fact that if anything even brushed up against my heel, I would scream, but *without* anything near the heel, I felt no pain and could walk *and run* normally.

So I did what any right-minded runner would do: I placed my running shoe on the kitchen island, used a Sharpie to outline on it the area that was hurting me, and asked my husband to *cut it out*.

He gave me a look and asked, "Cut what out?"

"The back of the shoe," I responded. "Please cut it out for me. My hand is not strong enough to cut through the plastic heel, and I need it out."

He realized I was serious. Very serious.

And he did it for me.

In that very shoe, I ran six miles and then five the next day, and I ran in it until my heel healed.

Running in that backless running-shoe has allowed me to think deeply about what else in my day, my life, or my social media might be pressing up against me and causing me pain or discomfort. *What else do I need to cut out?* I asked myself.

What in my day is constantly pressing on my time and, if I am honest, injuring me? I decided to take a keen look at my social media and what accounts I was following and what apps texted me to spend my first minutes on them, stealing more and more of my time.

Cutting it out began to look like unfollowing certain accounts, not because of what they were posting, but because of the heart I was hosting, because they made me feel bad or like I did not measure up or that I should be this way or that way. Cutting it out looked, for me, like placing certain apps on my smartphone on the second or third screen so they did not get priority in my sight and therefore in my mind and heart.

Cutting it out meant putting my phone on Do Not Disturb once the kids came home from school and having it always face down on the counter so that I could be present. It looked like not procrastinating and, instead, finishing a task to practice personal perseverance.

Does cutting it out mean not checking the latest updates first and instead getting into Scripture first thing in the morning to fill the space first with truth? Yes.

Does it mean not resorting to fear rather than faith when things get tough or scary? You bet.

Does it mean laying down resentments, worries, or hurts that are holding me back from joy? Yes, it does.

Does it mean turning up the volume on God's Word after turning down the volume on the voices (which tend to be our own) that echo condemnation and comparison? Does it mean filling up on the Word that encourages us and guides us, given to us by the One who created us? Absolutely. There are times I have been on the wrong path and needed to redirect completely. And then there are times we are on the right path and we just need to remove the hurtful heel.

I pray that God leads me and you to clearly decipher whether it is where we are headed or what is on our heel that needs to change. I pray that I can recognize that there are things keeping me from moving forward in the right direction and causing me pain with each step. I pray God gives me the courage to cut them out and make room for lots of grace, mercy, peace, gratitude, truth, trust, and joy. And I pray that when I am not strong enough to do that myself, He will always have Tim's strong hands and heart right by my side to do it for me.

Sometimes It Takes a Garbage Disposal

Speaking of Tim, by now you may know him as the rock of our family and the love of my life. We have had the blessing of knowing each other since my hair was brown and he had hair!

Our relationship began as friends and on trust. Being that I am a communicator with words, he usually knows where he stands with me. I am not the type to let him figure it out on his own.

Reading Gary Chapman's book *The Five Love Languages* years ago was one of the biggest catalysts in our relationship growth because it helped us identify how we each receive and give love. But communication did not always come easily about the little things.

For some reason, one evening about seven years into our marriage, I came up with the idea to "unpack" one thing each of us wanted the other to know. It sounded like a good plan for me to tell him what he was doing so he could fix it. Little did I realize that he would have a note for me too!

I finished telling him something small like, "It would be great if before I left for work, you told me I looked pretty and that I was going to do great." I needed the daily affirmation!

Then I said, "Your turn," almost positive he would say, "Oh, there is nothing you could do differently!"

He was quiet and then blurted out, *"The grape in the sink!"*

Silence. And shock.

He repeated, "The grape in the sink! You always leave a grape in the sink."

"I do?" I asked. I was baffled. I thought, *Every night I give the kids a bath, tuck them into bed, and say prayers with them. Then I race for the bunch of grapes in the fridge, rinse them, and sit with my research for the next day and read.* That was true.

My thoughts were interrupted when Tim said, "You always leave it in there for me to clean it up."

"I don't ever know it's there," I responded.

"That's because I reach into the drain every night and take it out and throw it away," he explained.

"You do?"

"Yes."

"Why?"

"Because it bugs me," he said.

"Then why don't you point it out to me in the moment so maybe I'd know it was there?" I paused, then asked, "Is this why you seem a little annoyed with me sometimes?"

It was a silly argument but a not-so-silly reminder that sometimes what can be small, like a grape in the sink, can become big if not communicated about properly. Since that conversation, we have opted for garbage disposals. On occasion, I still leave a grape in the sink or on Tim's nightstand just to make him laugh. But mostly, I make sure that I am not leaving things behind for him to deal with and that we bring up the "grapes in the sink"—those little things that might be driving us a little crazy—early enough that they never stand a chance to drive us apart, because we are on the same team. By covenant. As Mark 10:9 says, "Therefore what God has joined together, let no one separate."

Sometimes It Takes Crutches

This past year, Tim had knee surgery. Despite his determination during his recovery time, he was unable to do all the things he typically did. We learned a ton about our family team and ourselves during this season of slowing down. A change of plans for the summer meant a growth of heart. We realized that, instead of adventures on horses out west, being on crutches was what God had brought our tribe. Seeing the leader of our home leaning on crutches reminded us that we lean on one another and into the Word of God.

When Grace, Taylor, and Isaiah filled an ice machine for Tim or brought him water while he was doing his rehabilitation exercises on his leg, their actions blessed our home. We learned what it meant to serve the man who served our family so well every day. I learned that helping someone required not making him feel helpless.

Learning to anticipate what he could do each week, as well as what he could not do (and assisting him before he needed to ask for help), was crucial. We learned the importance of clearing the path. Clearing the path for Tim's time on crutches meant seeing the lay of the land before him and making it easier for him to get through the day. It meant picking up obstacles that would be in his way.

Hadn't I been doing this before he got hurt? Yes, sometimes. But it made me reflect on how much we can show our love for one another by clearing the path—smoothing the steps and taking out anything blocking progress for the one we care deeply about. I hope to take that with me and clear the path of Tim's day whenever it's within my ability. I want to make his day easier—perhaps by making the coffee, filling his car with gas occasionally, or taking on something he normally does to lighten his load. Clear the path for the person you love. Don't wait for crutches to see the strength of your heart.

Sometimes It Takes a Paintbrush

After coming out of *The View* and FOX and the trenches of early-morning news, finding my creative self again took a while. With painting and large-scale drawing being my college major, I knew that creativity was in me, but it had been set aside for a long season. Partly for motivation and partly as a self-dare, I purchased a few small canvases and a large canvas (thirty-six by forty-eight inches).

Thankfully our children are wildly creative and loved that I had those canvases ready to be filled up. One particular rainy day, we decided to set up a studio shop in the garage. Gathering up paint, old and new, and locating brushes and palette knives took longer than I thought. Once I had their area set up, and they were happily, creatively painting with music blasting, I stood in front of the massive empty canvas. Tim had helped me set up the easel so I could reach it from top to bottom.

Tim has always been a chief encourager for my creations, and I think at that point he wanted to see if I could still do it as much as I did. But more than that, he wanted me to feel the joy that came with painting. The girl he'd dated in college loved to paint, and in those days, I basically walked around in overalls splattered with color and a brush in my pocket, if I was not in eye black from my softball games.

That big white canvas seemed to taunt me as minutes went by and evaporated. The acrylic paint I had placed on the palette was drying by the time I got the courage to begin.

Any painter knows that prepping a canvas is the key to making your artwork last and to creating the ideal surface for your brushstrokes. I was so intimidated by starting again that I figured this painting would just be a sketch painting. Therefore, no preparation of the canvas was needed, as it was not going to turn out to be much of anything anyway. In fact, I was so uncertain about it that I decided that I would just study a still life object. *A pineapple,* I concluded. *That is what I will paint.*

The kids had long finished their masterpieces, and I was so enamored with the process and feel of painting again that I did not move out of that garage except to get them sandwiches for lunch at the midway point.

Eight hours later, a three-foot-tall pink pineapple was finished, and I stepped back. What had begun as a sketch became a finished piece, not because of what it was, but because I had tried.

In painting the pineapple, I began to think about each section, and how all I was doing was aiming to depict something God had already created. Mine could not be eaten or grilled; it couldn't smell sweet. I was simply redefining what He had created—so the pressure was actually off.

Sometimes when we want to try something for the first time again, we just need to paint the pineapple. We simply need to get a brush on the canvas, take the pressure off, and not worry about making the preparation or finished product perfect. Just start. Whatever your "pineapple" is, go ahead and start painting!

It Always Requires the Word

The experiences I share here happened by His power, not my might. By His grace, not by my grit. By His will, not my want. I just needed to use the right tool. His Word *is* the living tool He has given us, the tool that transforms us. The best news is that when Jesus went to heaven, He left us the Helper who inspired the Word of God, who is within us and gives us the tool for life. It is given to us because God wants us to use the right tool, His Word—by His power and through His Spirit—to get all the joy, all forty ounces in the jar of life.

For me, doing this at times seems complex. A word in the Bible can transform my heart? Really? Sometimes our children are the best way for me to see this happening.

One day after school, Taylor and Isaiah were outside playing. Anyone who has boys knows that it is all going well—until it isn't. Well, one slam dunk led to another, and someone said something to someone, and then it did not end well. But here was an opportunity for growth. I had told them that if they came to me to referee an argument, I was going to solve it by giving them some extra yard work.

Wisely, this time they decided that it was best to handle the situation on their own. It got quiet in the house, and usually that means trouble. I ran up the stairs calling their names, expecting them to be up to something. They were quietly in their rooms. I let them be. Later that day, long after the dust settled and many more games had been played and homework had been done, I asked them what they did when they were so mad and why it got so quiet in our home. They said they ran up to their rooms and opened their Bibles to the Help tab I had made, to a page that had different emotions and scriptures to read when feeling that emotion.

"I just flipped to the part that said 'When I Am Mad' and what to read. And I read that," one of my boys said.

With a surprised face, the other added, "It *actually* worked. Not right away, but after I read it, I was not *as* mad anymore. Isn't that weird?"

"Love, it is awesome," I responded. "It is awesome that you boys went there, went to the Word—and look what it did to your hearts."

Disclaimer: Before you mistakenly think you should send any Mom of the Year trophies my way, it's important to note we still have plenty of disagreements in my house. After all, they are normal kids. But I'm glad we have this particular instance to look back on as a positive way of approaching conflict resolution.

The power of the right tool is the gift of this great God to us—the God who knows that we cannot un-mad ourselves, un-pride ourselves, or un-sad ourselves. He gives us His Word, inspired by the Spirit, which, by the power of the Spirit, is able to transform our hearts.

11

Let's Have the Momversation

Now to him who is able to do immeasurably more than all we ask or imagine, according to his power that is at work within us, to him be glory in the church and in Christ Jesus throughout all generations, for ever and ever! Amen.

—Ephesians 3:20–21

W e have little tiny hearts in our midst—hearts that ask us questions and need protection, love, direction, and correction. Let's not take these hearts lightly, but let's also not proceed without soaking in the permission to do this that comes from above. It comes from God. He spoke it, and we are moms. So let's not underestimate the calling and not overestimate our capabilities without His power.

I am still learning this the hard way. But one thing I do know: these children God has placed in our care came with a responsibility—to love them and to point their eyes to Him.

Being able to be real with each other when it comes to this awesome calling is a gift—being real and being really vulnerable in our mistakes. I have made some big ones. It happens. And I'm pretty sure it doesn't only happen to me. All moms make mistakes sometimes, and being able to share them in a momversation makes the journey easier and makes us stronger.

Anyone who knows me well knows I tend to be a bit of a pack rat. I like to have a lot of "just in case" items with me. This is so well known among my friends that when someone needs a Band-Aid or a snack or a stapler, they come to me because chances are I have one in my tote.

I'm always impressed with the fact that my husband can leave the house with just his wallet, his keys, and his phone. We women sometimes carry so much with us. I can remember having the diaper bag stockpiled as if I needed to leave the country on a moment's notice. I was ready for anything. Sometimes "arming up" with the just-in-case items made me feel ready to handle the unexpected. Perhaps living in New York City is partly to blame. As a pedestrian stroller mom, your stroller and your bag are what get you from point to point all day long. I want to carry less in my bag—and less on my heart. The amazing thing is that I am realizing that the more I am in the Word and the more of the Word I hold, the less room I have for all the stuff.

As moms, we learn to carry. We carry our babies, their binkies, their bottles, their snacks, their diapers. We carry sparkling water—and a lot more. We carry the worries of our kids, the shame of our mistakes, and the hope that things will be better. We carry the burden for the child in our home or the job that we have or the hours that seem to be less for us than someone else. We carry the questions: How does she get all that done? Why am I so behind? Will I ever be enough?

We carry the striving instead of thriving.

Whether we are working moms or stay-at-home moms, we are all full-time moms. So let's have the momversation about mompensation, which is overcompensating for what we feel we have messed up with the best intentions of getting it right for our kids.

Every Day Can Be the First Day for Grace

We tend to figure a lot out the hard way on our firstborn. Mine is the strongest girl I know, and that has nothing to do with how much I have done right. Case in point: our little girl, Grace, was so excited for her first day of school. We celebrated the last day of summer with some friends in the park. The anticipation was building for Grace's first day of school ever.

Then the phone rang and a serious-yet-concerned tone greeted my ear: "Hello. Mrs. Hasselbeck? This is So-and-So School, and we are calling just to make sure that Grace will be joining us this year."

"Of course," I replied, doubly impressed that they were giving courtesy calls and reminders. "Grace is so excited! She has her lunch box all set out, and her bow, and we can't wait to meet everyone on the first day tomorrow!"

Then came the pause that I have heard comes before an avalanche.

"Mrs. Hasselbeck, the first day of school was today."

I don't even remember saying goodbye to the caller or hanging up, because I could have sworn there was suddenly a total solar eclipse. And the scream that I thought I had to let out in Central Park would have warranted the NYPD immediately galloping into the playground where we were.

But the scream—that loud shaming scream—was not heard because it was on the inside: "How did we forget the first day of school?"

It was her first day of school—*ever*.

And the "we" that I was rolling around in my mind really meant "me." How could *I* have missed the most important day in my three-and-a-half-year-old's entire life?

The big bow, the monogrammed lunch box, the ruffle socks, the seersucker dress—nothing I had prepared ahead of time mattered. We—meaning *me*—had failed.

Then shame set in. And the mompensation began.

I had to make it better.

The next day I took Grace's "first"-day-of-school picture outside our apartment. I walked her through the doors of the school, getting looks from the administration (some of excitement and some weighted with judgment). No matter how anyone else looked at me, nothing compared to the shame and disappointment I had in myself.

When I kissed Grace goodbye and said, "Have a great first day of school!" a little boy said, "It's actually the second day of school."

"Well, it's the first day for Grace!" I said.

I went home that morning and started mompensating, desperate to get it all right. But I needed the reminder from God that every day can be the first day for grace if we kick out shame with the truth of what God has created us to be as moms.

But for me, this first day for grace has been forgotten sometimes. And no matter how many times I remind myself of it, I have to remind myself again. Perhaps that goes back to that walk-on mentality: If I was late to practice, I had a four-in-the-morning running punishment workout. If I missed a ball, I did sit-ups. I am all for appropriate consequences, but I think I had gotten into the bad habit of not letting go of something after the resolution.

Even when it comes to my identity in Christ, I sometimes fall back on not letting the debt be paid, not remembering that Christ died on the cross so I could live forever. I still have to shake the natural tendency to take the consequence, run the sprints, and shed the shame or blame that goes with failure. God desires more for us. But what pushes me could plague me. My desire to work so hard and earn it or make it right has a very real limit. And His has none. Every day is a first day for grace.

Failing the Rest Test

I will admit that, until just recently, I pridefully fell back on seeing God as my reserve tank. My perspective was, He knows when I can work hard, and then, for the things I don't have a handle on, He helps me out. He is a great pinch runner.

Sounds like a great setup, right? Not really.

Especially during my time on *FOX & Friends,* I had surrendered all that I thought I could not handle alone—talking about terror and Afghanistan and the backlash that comes when you take any position on any topic. As I wrote earlier, I worked with the most incredible team at FOX and loved the entire crew. The decision to walk away from my position there was hard but clear.

I was on my knees before the start of every day, begging God to carry me through it, because I knew I could not do it on my own. I gave up. But I did not give it over. And there is a difference. That was a problem. Giving *up* opens your hands and releases the problem. Giving it *over* opens your hands and grasps for God to take control of the challenges and hold us while we move through the turbulent times.

I left the job and traded in morning news to become Chief Breakfast Officer, and then came the lie: "I've got this now," I told God. "Thanks for the help with terror and war and hard news and early wake-ups. That was hard. Whew! But now—this home stuff is easy, right? I've got it now. You can come back in when something big comes up."

I had made the tough decision. I had changed course, and this time I knew who was in the lead, but the haunting walk-on way took over, came back, and was having a good ol' time with me.

On my first morning at home, I thought, *I've got this.* With that came the expectation: Mommy's home now. Things are going to be perfect. I've got this!

My sweet girl was urging the boys to hurry through their morning routine, a flurry of activity that looked so unfamiliar to me and had gotten blurry over the previous two years.

Do they have vitamins after breakfast or before? I wondered.

A feeling of rush was in the air. No one was happy, expectations were falling, I was making breakfast, and we were running behind. And my daughter was trying to keep everything on track.

"Grace is rushing me!" one of my boys said.

In a moment of gross reaction, I looked at her and said, "Grace, why are you rushing everyone around this morning? I'm finally home, and everything is stressful for some reason. All your rushing is ruining the morning!"

Verbal arrows.

I stopped. I stood broken at that kitchen table and prayed a prayer that I thought I only needed when I was stranded in the middle of the Australian outback, when I was having surgery, when I was exhausted driving to a job for which I felt unqualified and undeserving of in the dark hours of the morning: *Father God, please help me. Jesus, be with me. I need You now like never before. Please use me for Your glory today. I need You.*

I looked across the table at Grace with tears in my eyes—and saw tears in her eyes. "Grace, I am so, so sorry," I said. "This is what you *have had to do* with Mommy gone in the mornings, isn't it?"

Her look said, *Well, someone had to.*

"Grace, I'm here now," I told her. "Take off that backpack of responsibility, that feeling that it is all on you, and give it over to Mommy. That is not yours to carry. It's mine."

When I realized I had fully surrendered that but had not fully rested in the fact that God holds everything I should have had a handle on—being a mom, being a wife—then certainly the Monday morning breakfast thing should have felt easier, right?

It should have felt more peaceful, but the rest I had sought was nowhere to be found because rest, for me, meant being lazy, not doing enough, or being asleep. But biblically speaking, to rest means to lean on, to trust, to sit in the comfort of another, to stop. I had to stop the lie that said, "You've got this. Work hard and get it."

Now I know that REST means Releasing Everything in Surrender To God.

I had it all wrong. I thought I was "well rested," but resting on God's promises means more than relaxing on the sofa or sleeping nine hours each night (though sleep is important).

I can look back now and see that what I was asking in taking the backpack from Grace is exactly what God is asking of us every moment of every day. The difference is Christ has already taken it for us. Isaiah 30:15 says, "This is what the Sovereign LORD, the Holy One of Israel, says: 'In repentance and rest is your salvation, in quietness and trust is your strength, but you would have none of it.'"

Releasing Everything in Surrender To God

Let's look at this one word at a time.
- *Releasing.* That's not easy for me.
- *Everything.* What I was still holding on to (because I had it!) was the very thing that made me most vulnerable. Sometimes there's something we will not release to God because we are too scared we will not get the answer we want or we believe that we have a handle on it. *Everything* means *everything.*
- *Surrender.* We surrender by His power, not ours.
- *To God.* This is a one-way mailing. We give it all to Him, and there is no return address, because our tendency is to mail it with a self-addressed stamped return envelope. When we surrender something, we don't take it back.

I think it's a good idea for all of us to repeat these words often: "*God is not my pinch runner. I don't need Him sometimes. I need Him all the time.*"

In the moment when Grace looked at me through tears and realized she did not have to carry the weight of that backpack, I saw a little girl who was free. Just as I, the parent, delighted in wanting nothing more than for her to be lightened by surrendering the burdens that were not hers, our heavenly Father wants us to hand over our backpacks to Him—completely.

Misunderstanding rest is exactly what the devil wants us to do. He wants us not to feel the comfort of leaning back into the arms of the Father above and the freedom that comes with it. He wants us locked in uncertainty, locked in our own will, locked in our expectations, locked in our capabilities, and locked in the failure that comes with doing it on our own. He wants us in the business of letting everyone—and ourselves—down and of not letting go.

Ask yourself today: Where is the one place you feel like you've got it? The one place that you have it so under control that you know right now you don't even need to surrender the reins because you are saying to yourself, "I so have this."

Why would I ask you to acknowledge that one thing? Because that is the area in which evil will attempt to get you tangled up.

So give that one to God. Find your rest.

Know that God looks at you as a daughter of a king—priceless, beloved, forgiven—and says, "Stop acting as if you have to carry this all on your own." Every time we say and think, "I've *so* got this," we take it out of our Father's hand.

Next time you find yourself faced with the *lie*—"I've got this"—

remember that it comes with the *challenge* of misunderstanding rest and not being fully surrendered. Then comes the *promise:* you don't have to have it because God does.

Locating the Manual

Clearly, as I have shared in the above stories, we malfunction sometimes. We mess up. We make mistakes. But that does not mean we are a mistake. Missteps are an opportunity to search for the manual on how to get ourselves fully functioning again. Find the manual.

When an appliance in my house malfunctions, I search the house and search online for the manufacturer's manual. I go straight to the source—the maker, the manufacturer—and ask how to make the appliance function well again.

God is our maker. Why does it take me longer to go to my own manufacturer than to the manufacturer of my blender or mixer when it is not working right? Mommas, we have the manual in our homes and hands and online—the Word of God. Most importantly, God gave it to us by His Spirit in our hearts. Having the same manual means we have the same maker. We can do this because we are *made* to do it. But not without turning to that awesome manufacturer and His flawless direction.

Go Climb a Tree with Them

Let's turn up the fun and participation with our kids. Let's think about what makes them smile. Taylor loves to fish. And I love Taylor, so I hit the sports store, pick out some bait and a tackle box, and we go to the pond together.

Isaiah loves to paint, so I like to have some canvases on hand and some paint and brushes ready to go—and we do that together. He loves to cook, so we tackle a recipe together.

Grace loves to draw and loves to play the guitar, so we drive to the guitar store, and she teaches me about what kind of pick she likes because I don't speak guitar.

Thankfully, all my children like to play catch, and that I can still do!

Whenever one of them has entered a growth time, I have taken them to a ropes course. There is something about being tethered together up in the trees that bonds us and grows us. Mostly, we share the experience of wondering if we can make it from point A to point B. We are on the same level. I begin by going first, leading the way. By the middle of the course, I let them lead. This is the point in the day when I am getting tired and more scared (because I am over forty!), and they are getting more confident and energized by that confidence. So I let them lead. What begins as me encouraging them ends with them instructing me and encouraging me to use the best technique to get across and not fall.

I had no idea when I first did a ropes course with Grace what it would do for our relationship. Now, having taken Grace, Taylor, and Isaiah—all at those times when we were leaving one post in life and about to climb, in essence, to another—it has proven to be the best physical and emotional bond for us.

As a dad, Tim has made something with each of our children over time, something of use and something our family has needed—a shelf, a bench, a gate—something that takes time and teamwork. Sanding, nailing, and installing together has brought a smoothness, a security, and a place in heart and home for each of them with him.

I think the most important ingredient in our family life is time spent doing something together. This may change over time, but so far it works for us.

Let Them Write on the Walls and Their Hands

"TAYLOR THOMAS HASSELBECK! I *told* you not to write on your hands!"

He looked up at me with reddened cheeks and wide eyes. He held a Sharpie in one hand and made a fist with the other hand. I had told them not to write on their hands.

"Open your hand right now, and show me what was so important that you needed to permanently write it inside your hand!" I demanded.

A gulp and a gradually opening fist revealed: "I ♥ MOM."

And in an instant, I smiled, and he smiled, and we laughed and hugged tight.

"Taylor, you can write on your hands like that all you want. Mommy was wrong about that rule."

To see a son's love for me on the palm of his hand was pure joy. It was his expression of affection, in a place that meant so much to him. If you get to know our Taylor, you'll learn that he has super strong hands and a strong loyal heart. That moment I felt held by him—his heart and his hands.

After all, God wrote His love for us on His hands—on the palms of His only Son.

Banning the Command to Hurry Up

There was a time when I found myself in a rhythm of rushing my kids when I was actually the one rushing. "Hurry up" was just something I said. It became a bad habit—until one day I slowed down enough to see what I was missing.

It was a day leading up to my surgery while I was working at FOX News, and everything was being crammed into the week. Perhaps I was aiming to stock up on fun because I thought I would be laid up in bed recovering for a while. Maybe I thought that if I overscheduled the week, no one would notice or worry about my upcoming procedure. Including me.

That whole week, I hurried to work, and they hurried to school, and we hurried home to hurry up and wash our hands to hurry up and get outside and play. I hurried up to get dinner, and they hurried up to finish homework, and we hurried up with the bath to hurry up before bedtime.

One day I was trying to get the kids in the car for a basketball-shooting clinic, and the clock was moving way faster than our pace. As I gathered Gatorade bottles and bags and one more snack for the trip, the words *Hurry up* were on the tip of my tongue.

But the words stayed on my tongue and did not breathe out, because on the floor of the garage was my son trying so hard to tie his shoe with his little fingers. We would be late if he didn't hurry up. But being on time for this practice was going to have to wait because something precious was happening before my eyes, and God gave me the Pause button to see it. Why would I have hurried him through this tender moment—his hard work, his diligent heart, his sweaty brow? And all it took was taking the dare to slow down enough to stop and watch something precious unfold. That day something changed in me. I made a promise to not "hurry up" my kids through life. I made a promise not to say it until I did not feel it, and it helped. It helped me not overschedule each day so I wouldn't feel so tight on time. And it helped me not overpack my heart, making me realize that I had room to stop and see that there was nothing more important or big to my little boy than finally tying his shoelaces without his momma holding a stopwatch.

Encourage One Another Daily

There is not a game, concert, debate, birthday, or big event for our family that doesn't inspire our youngest, Isaiah, to make a sign. "Let's go!" "You've got this!" Usually, lots of illustrations, fun writing, and glued additions adorn the sign.

When we get to that game or activity, we know for sure there is someone rooting for us . . . and that someone is Isaiah. His encouragement through art and in his poster sign language is such a gift to us. It is also a reminder that *knowing someone is for you* matters.

The rest of us have since taken on his habit, and we try to make signs saying that we are for each other. After all, Hebrews 3:13 tells us to encourage one another daily. Isaiah reminds us that we are to be one another's biggest fans. If Isaiah could walk down each morning with face paint and a T-shirt for all of us, he would. He treats every day as if it is the Super Bowl and we are the team he is rooting for. His instrument of affection is something we love to receive, and it has exemplified to us the importance of daily encouragement for our team and others.

Spotting Character

Our family friend Michael Erwin who founded Team RWB also founded a nonprofit organization called the Positivity Project, www.posproject.org. Its mission is "empowering students to build positive relationships," and #OtherPeopleMatter is their hashtag.

Clinging to our family's chalk calendar is a magnet from the Positivity

Project that lists twenty-four character strengths, with an icon for each one. Identifying each of these and learning about which ones we naturally excel in or are gifted in, as well as areas we need to work on as members of our family, has been wildly instrumental in how we communicate and relate with one another. I witnessed the Positivity Project firsthand in a school I visited in North Carolina, where bullying had been an issue until they included this program in the curriculum. I listened as two middle school girls talked to me about how they disliked each other prior to learning about their character strengths and weaknesses.

"I thought she was too loud, and it always bothered me that she always raised her hand with questions in class, but now I know that her top character strengths are leadership and curiosity," said one.

Her friend smiled and said to me, "And I just thought she was rude and judgmental because she always sat in the same spot and never spoke. But now I know that her character strengths are discipline and justice."

They went from being enemies to being friends because they saw each other's character. I realized that if this could work between classmates, it would surely work in our home! Our goal is to have the kids "spot" one of the strengths when they see it during their days in school, with their friends, at the store, and in our home. The goal for Tim and me is to spot it when we see it in them. It has given us a reason and a language for talking about the actions and words. We are seeing the person. And we are seeing relationships strengthen and deepen because we are seeing each other's hearts.

There's Always Time for a Momversation

I am thankful to have the momversation anytime! We moms are not in this alone, and there is power in numbers. Your friends are there, placed by God to walk with you through parenting, marriage, and trials. He gave you these mommas to share life with and to entrust your heart to. I am so thankful to the women around me, the walks and talks. They refocus my eyes on God's power and mighty hand, not ours.

Do I believe that He has it, whatever "it" is in our lives at any given time? Do I believe that He holds our children, and we hold them, and He holds us? I have to.

Do I believe He has a unique purpose for each of our children? Yes.

Do I believe He will give us strength when we need it? Yes.

I have seen it in other moms. We walk and we talk. We have laughed and cried. We are compelled to do fun things with our kids for a reason. We do not have to decide to be observers; we can participate with them.

In the mom fails I shared in this chapter, I resisted surrendering to the fact that these children are on loan to me. I have realized that I need to hand over the reins to the One who reigns. As I do that, I need to also proceed with the confidence that He has commissioned me to do this very thing.

A Prayer for Moms

Dear God, thank You for these children that You let us parent. God, let us turn to You, Your Word, Your wisdom, as You are the Father of all fathers. Let Your unconditional love for us be the marker of our love for our children. God, give us the confidence that comes with knowing that You are holding us as we hold them. Amen.

12

It's Party Time!

❧

If we really want to love, we must learn how to forgive.

—MOTHER TERESA

During the fall of 2017, I threw my kids a party. It wasn't a birthday. It wasn't a holiday. It was just a Monday. I didn't throw the party because I'm a perfect mom. On the contrary, I threw it because I'm not perfect at all. And my daughter and two sons got a front-row, Sunday matinee seat to my imperfection.

The week before that Sunday night was a tough one. For starters, I was behind on the list of things that should have been done already. Maybe I overlisted (quite possible). Or maybe I overstressed about all the items on my list. The pressure of having more things to do than I had time for had gotten to me. In addition, the week was filled with tears and heartache. We felt as if we were moving through the mud of mourning and grief for two little children we had come to love and called friends. Both lost their battles with sickness here on earth. Despite knowing they were ultimately healed in heaven and rejoicing that they felt no more pain there, our loss hit us hard in practical ways. I ached for their families and for my family because of the void we felt without them. My mom tank was brimming with stress, weariness, and emotional pain, and by that Sunday night, I was running seriously low on vitamin P—patience.

As our family sat around the kitchen table that night, in the midst of chicken nuggets, a ketchup bottle, and my emotional reserve tank on low—it happened. Someone hurt someone's feelings, and someone hurt someone else's arm. And I had had it.

After a brief attempt to use my calm, patient mom voice (I promise that I did attempt to locate it. It *had* to be somewhere since I had just used it seventeen times), all that came out of me was the plain old ugly loud voice. In a moment of weakness, I chose losing my patience over finding my grace.

I asked the kids to be patient and kind toward one another, and almost as quickly as that request crossed my lips, I realized that the very patience I was asking them to pinpoint and use was absent in me. The tone of voice I wanted them to use with each other was nothing like the tone with which I spoke to them. In their faces, I saw tenderness, curiosity, and the question: *Why does Mom demand patience and kindness from us when she is acting like a momster?*

"What is a momster?" you ask. Well, a momster is when a mom gets an ugly face while using her less-than-graceful volume due to sheer human limitations and low patience supply—most often occurring right after homework and before dinnertime.

I had to give the kids credit. Their wondering was perfectly reasonable.

Realizing this hypocrisy as words tumbled out of my mouth at greater speed and greater volume than I would ever be proud to re-enact, I stopped right in my tracks. With less momster face and more sobster face, I fell to my knees next to the kids. I could not hold back the tears as I spoke to them, "I am so, so very sorry that Mommy lost her patience. Please forgive me. I love you with my whole heart, and there is nothing that should steal my patience. I'm sorry. Forgive me, lovies. Mommy just lost her grace. Please forgive me."

And do you know what?

They did.

They forgave me fully and joyfully.

Just. Like. That.

They forgave me. They didn't have to. I didn't make them—I couldn't make them. They didn't wait for me to be perfect before they extended their forgiveness. They just did it. And the night got a reset.

Before we all went to bed, we snuggled and read some books we loved. I apologized a couple thousand more times just in case—and we fell asleep. The next morning, I woke up, loved on the kids even more than my usual goopy ways, and got them to school singing along with our favorite songs. Yesterday was yesterday. All the negativity of Sunday evening was gone.

Or So I Thought

I can still remember the thud of the car door that morning as the kids hopped out for school and waved goodbye to me as they balanced their backpacks on one shoulder and offered one more smile. As each child exited the car, I felt the fresh fall air, but that was not all. With it, guilt, shame, and condemnation invited themselves into the car, buckled their seat belts, and annoyingly decided to ride along with me everywhere I went.

I could not see them, but oh, could I ever hear them: *What kind of a mommy would have to ask her kids to forgive her? How hard would it have been for you to be just a little more patient?* And the sarcastic jab, *Way to go, Mom of the Century!*

All I could do was keep driving, eyes on the road, mind battling as hard as it could against the noise.

The shame, guilt, and self-condemnation stayed in their seats, filling the air in the car, intent on making me feel bad about something I thought I had already dealt with. I thought I had moved on, but the lies kept nipping at my mind. The condemnation crept back into my heart, and before

I knew it, I was reminded of the volume of my voice the night before—and of its harsh tone. A fresh wave of disappointment over the situation on Sunday evening washed over me. Despite their tireless efforts to gain occupancy in my mind, they could not because no matter how they pursued me, my God pursued me more.

I could feel this happening. A battle. And God was going to win.

So I prayed: *God, I know You lightened our hearts yesterday. Please help me not still feel bad today. Please help me forgive me again. Please help me feel light about this. I know it was just an impatient night with the kids, but it feels like I am still the worst person right now.*

What was that scripture I just read in a devotional yesterday? I asked myself. *"Therefore, there is now no condemnation for those who are in Christ Jesus." Yes! Romans 8:1.* That was exactly what I needed to hear!

I remembered John 3:17: "For God did not send his Son into the world to condemn the world, but to save the world through him." How much did I believe that?

For years I read the Bible as a remedy after a challenge came up—or a hardship, a mistake, a disappointment—and surely after failure. Now I read before, during, and after the challenges! Here is the deal: the good, the bad, the ugly, the horrible, and the wonderful *will* happen. Putting on the armor of God (using His Word to strengthen you while in the battle you face) is a good thing. Putting it on *before* something happens—because it will—is a great thing. It will not take the challenge away, but you will feel ready for the battle that is coming your way.

An everyday example of preparing for the battle is the habit my husband has of getting his coffee ready for the next morning the night before. He sets a timer on the coffeepot so that the coffee is already made when he gets up. He knows that his cup of coffee will help him feel more awake and ready for the day at hand. In this same way, we can arm up and prepare for what is coming next in our lives, knowing that "in this world you will have trouble" (John 16:33). That is true.

Since I know I will face difficulties, shouldn't I prepare my armor of God as well? Shouldn't I have it ready to be put on the next day? Shouldn't I get Scripture percolating through my mind? I could wait for the caffeine headache to set in and then make coffee, suffering in the time between the headache's onset and the first sip of coffee. But I would be wise to arm up beforehand with the knowledge that I'm going to need something to get me through the day.

As I remembered the words of Romans 8:1 and John 3:17, God gave me the words to cover the lies of guilt, shame, and condemnation. He gave me the guideposts for a road to victory. I remembered His instructions: "Set your minds on things above, not on earthly things" (Colossians 3:2). His words began to crowd out the lies with truth. Soon there was no room in my car, in my mind, or in my heart for lies. And by the power of the Holy Spirit, guilt and shame took a hike for the day.

Filling up on God's truth, His Word, leaves little room for the lies of anyone else to occupy real estate in our hearts. But it is up to us to read and protect ourselves with truth. We need to get into the truth early and often.

I recalled how our three children forgave me, extended grace to me when I lacked it, and loved me even when I was far from loveable. I remembered how they actually smiled a bit when I asked them to be the forgivers, as if to say, *Well, this is nice for a change, since we are always the ones having to say "I'm sorry" all the time!*

I was so excited that I thought about picking up all the kids from school and giving them a half day off. Frankly, I wanted their affirmations. I wanted to feel close to them, and they were not scheduled to be home for seven hours. But taking them out of school seemed disruptive and a little selfish. With a fresh heart, I went with my backup plan:

A party.

That's what we would do. An ice cream party. But not just any party. When they got home from school, I would throw them . . . a forgiveness party! Our family favorites—black raspberry chip, mint chocolate chip, and Graeter's Buckeye Blitz—were piled into my cart!

When I returned home, I made notes that said, "The only thing sweeter than Graeter's ice cream is forgiveness" and "We forgive because He forgave us first." I flipped through ABC Scripture cards made by my friend Courtney DeFeo and found a verse for the letter *B:* "Be kind and compassionate to one another, forgiving each other" (Ephesians 4:32). The scripture cards have been a staple on our kitchen island or countertop for years, and they have cookie dough and pasta spots on them to prove it! This momma needs all the reminders of God's truth she can get—more of His point of view, less of mine.

When my party preparation frenzy calmed down a bit, I looked at the pages I had marked in Jeannie Cunnion's book *Mom Set Free* and reread the part about moms not having to be perfect for our kids: "Our job is not to *be* God; it's to point our children *to* God."

I prayed over Ephesians 2:8–9 to keep myself grounded in the fact that this party was being thrown not to *get* grace and forgiveness but to celebrate that *by* the grace of God we are forgiven! "For it is by grace you have been saved, through faith—and this is not from yourselves, it is the gift of God—not by works, so that no one can boast."

When the kids came home from school and dropped their backpacks, they saw the full party mode in our kitchen and asked with a mix of curiosity and excitement, "What's this for!?"

With a smile, I answered, "It's a party. Because you forgave me."

Then my youngest asked a question that gave me the greatest relief: "Forgave you for what?"

I could hardly believe I had to remind him: "For messing up last night and using a big loud voice. Remember? But you forgave me and today is new, and it feels like a party when you are forgiven. I am so thankful and so happy to be forgiven, I thought I would throw one for us."

"Awesome!" the kids said.

"Mommy?" My son looked up with a witty smile. "Can you mess up *more*?"

I knew the answer to that immediately. "Um, yes, lovey. I'm *pretty* sure I can do that."

The only thing sweeter than my absolute favorite ice cream is the forgiveness my kids served me that day.

We're All Invited

Reflecting on the party and on how much the kids enjoyed it, I realize it's impossible to tell that story and not share how much *I* enjoyed it and how much it meant to me. The whole situation helped me see so much more clearly how God sees me in those situations. I don't have to be perfect because He is. My kids forgave me, and the joy that comes with that forgiveness called for a party. The joy that comes with trusting that we have a forgiving God is worth a party too!

When it comes to forgiveness, what exactly is God's point of view? It's worth a look at several scriptures that help sharpen our focus.

For God so loved the world that he gave his one and only Son,
that whoever believes in him shall not perish but have eternal life.
(John 3:16)

But you, Lord, are a compassionate and gracious God, slow
to anger, abounding in love and faithfulness. (Psalm 86:15)

But God demonstrates his own love for us in this: While we
were still sinners, Christ died for us. (Romans 5:8)

No, in all these things we are more than conquerors through
him who loved us. For I am convinced that neither death nor
life, neither angels nor demons, neither the present nor the
future, nor any powers, neither height nor depth, nor anything
else in all creation, will be able to separate us from the love of
God that is in Christ Jesus our Lord. (Romans 8:37–39)

But because of his great love for us, God, who is rich in mercy,
made us alive with Christ even when we were dead in transgressions—it is by grace you have been saved. (Ephesians 2:4–5)

This is how God showed his love among us: He sent his one and
only Son into the world that we might live through him. This is
love: not that we loved God, but that he loved us and sent his Son
as an atoning sacrifice for our sins. (1 John 4:9–10)

My great hope and prayer is that you will join the party of God's
forgiveness and freedom, breathing out the peace and joy that come with
it. If you are struggling to move forward under the weight of something
you have done or said, some way you have hurt the people around you, or
maybe some regret you simply cannot get past, I want you to know that
this is not an invitation only for the person who has checked off all life's
boxes. The invitation to this party is for *you*. You can be forgiven and

free—free from the guilt, embarrassment, and misery that come with making mistakes. It's as simple as confessing the sin, asking for forgiveness, and believing you are forgiven—because the Bible says you are.

Forgiveness Math

Sometimes we cannot see God's invitation because our math is wrong. I used to think the forgiveness equation went like this:

a wrong + an apology = forgiveness

In other words, Person A wrongs Person B. That wrong subtracts something from Person B. Person A then adds an apology and that equals forgiveness.

After all, I wondered, how could forgiveness happen without a proper apology? It's simple math, isn't it? Wrong. In fact, we waste our time, our hearts, and our emotions when we wait for a "deserved apology" or explanation of wrongdoing.

But when we forgive anyway, when we forgive His way, we no longer subtract freedom from our hearts. Dr. Lewis Smedes tells us why in his book *Forgive and Forget:* "You set a prisoner free, but you discover that the real prisoner was yourself."

Forgiveness is ours to give because it has been given to us already! Ephesians 4:32 provides this clear instruction, "Be kind and compassionate to one another, forgiving each other, just as in Christ God forgave you." When we see and believe that we have forgiveness to offer others because it was first extended to us, we can share that forgiveness with others. When we realize that we were forgiven before we apologized, before we even realized our actions against another person were wrong, before we hurt someone, before we offended a friend or family member. Before everything, we were forgiven.

Sometimes forgiveness happens seamlessly and easily. It's as though everything about it converged in the right way—people's hearts and minds, the timing, the place. People decided to forgive each other, and then they moved on.

Sometimes forgiveness isn't seamless, it isn't easy, and it doesn't look like we want it to at all. For example, offering forgiveness rarely brings back an estranged family member right away. The reunion might not ever take place on this earth. Rebuilding a relationship that has been severed for months or years takes time. Forgiveness might bring that person back eventually, but it's not a magic potion that will make him or her suddenly reappear, smiling and happy. Extending forgiveness doesn't promise to make people who harmed you regret how much they hurt you. More likely, it will not. They still may not care, but at least your heart will not still ache.

What forgiveness *does* do is point a person—the one who forgives and even possibly the one who is forgiven—back to Christ. Forgiveness is an offering without an expectation, an offering that prays deeply that hearts would change, not because we have forgiven but because of what God has done, who He is, and what He can do in His perfect timing. Forgiveness is not the end of trouble, pain, or suffering. It is the beginning of repair and rejoicing and of the freedom that comes in the heart of the one who forgives.

The math is complex. I've learned over the years that it is far more complicated than having an offense and an apology equal perfection. I've also learned that the tricky forgiveness equation is not up to us to solve. We might scribble it out or try to make it work, and God understands that. But in the end, He is the one who holds the eraser, the one who causes the pain of offense to vanish in our hearts. Not us.

In order to really forgive, we have to do it God's way. I know this because for years I tried to do it my way, and I failed. All that happens when we try to do it on our own terms is that we get more pain, more suffering, more anxiety, more frustration—and way less freedom.

I'll admit that sometimes I still want forgiveness to operate as I think it should. Don't we all? A+B = C. Done.

Solving problems and fixing mistakes can make me feel better. Ideally, those mistakes would be erased until the marks on the paper cannot be seen anymore. But the math of heaven says the clean paper is not mine to create. It is actually mine to receive because God is the eraser of all the smudges, not me.

13

Mama's Meatballs:
Tastes of Heaven

Just a taste . . .

—MAMA

Mama (my mom's mom) used to make sauce and meatballs every Sunday. Typically, when I slept at her house on a Saturday night, we would watch *The Golden Girls* and brush each other's hair. I would help her vacuum and dust, and she would cook. Mama was up early every morning. She grew tomatoes, basil, and zucchini and would ripen them occasionally on her windowsill.

On Sundays, she woke up before I did and prayed, devoted to her time with Jesus. By the time I woke up, the smell of meat and sauce was already permeating the house. As I helped her get ready for the big Sunday supper, I would pop over to the counter to peer at the big pot of goodness. Mama would always take out a meatball and some sauce early and give me a taste before anyone else. It was a hint of what was to come later, a heavenly taste of the goodness she had prepared for us. All day long, I would await the main meal and rest in the fact that no matter what the day held, our whole family would be at the table together enjoying those meatballs!

Similarly, I believe God gives us heavenly tastes along the journey of life—glimpses of what heaven will be like—just when we need them or when we don't even realize we need them! Mama's meatballs were that to me, and I can see now how God has given me "meatballs," heavenly tastes, some of which I will share here.

Dancing with Cade

Dancing with Cade and a community of joyful hearts was unmistakably one of my top meatball moments. Cade is the oldest son of Rebekah and Gabe Lyons, and I get to call him "friend." My connection and friendship with him is much like my friendship with his mom. It is just meant to be, and I feel most myself when I am with him.

I remember getting ready for Night to Shine, a prom-night experience for young people with special needs. Focused on God's love, Night to Shine is sponsored by the Tim Tebow Foundation and hosted by churches. I picked out a dress, made plans with Cade's mom and dad, and got my hair done especially for the evening. Night to Shine is a night when hearts gather and heaven comes down.

As Cade approached the front door, he held in his hand a wrist corsage just for me. He was such a gentleman, and I told my boys as they stood by my side to take notes from this fine young man. We took our version of "pics" and drove to the dance. But the dancing started early. At every stoplight, we played a different song in the car and danced to it, smiling the whole way.

Once at the Night to Shine entrance, we walked the red carpet, and we both felt the peace and joy of God there. Dancing with Cade was pure joy. The pastor of the church that hosted the event said that it "felt like heaven" and that "heaven came down." He was spot-on, as that taste of what heaven will be like one day—dancing with pure joy—was real.

It was a night when I didn't want tomorrow to come. I remember keeping my shoes on, hoping that if I kept them on, the night would last longer. It was just a taste, and I praise God for such a night.

Haiti with Grace

When a child leads your heart, you can tell you are about to get a taste of heaven. My brother-in-law was taking his wife, Sarah, one of my best friends, and their two daughters to Haiti to be at Danita's Children. They were so kind to extend the invitation also to Grace and me, knowing that we had longed to get there. The only issue was that they were going in a week.

Could we be ready?

Matthew invited us on a hot summer day, so I called outside to Grace, "Grace! Matthew and Sarah and Annabelle and Mallory are going to Danita's next week in Haiti—and they invited us. It would be next Wednesday. What do you think?" Their invitation was one of the most beautiful I have ever received.

Without missing a beat, she replied, "Haiti, with my cousins and Miss Karris and her boys, next week? Heck, yeah!"

I know God allowed me to ask her what she thought so I could hear her heart out loud. He knew I needed to be led by her heart. I would never have timed it that way. God just made room in the month and timed it so perfectly that even she would feel His awesome permission and enthusiasm to go.

Immunizations and packing lists, travel documents, prayers . . . Packing is not my strong suit and making the trip without my husband seemed intimidating at times. As I packed, I paused, first looking at my empty suitcase, then praying, then overpacking—and then God stopped me in my tracks and laid this on my heart to pray aloud: "God, unpack my heart. And empty it of all my worry and expectation. Unpack our hearts, God, so you can fill them with all you want in them."

He did just that, and oh, did He give Grace and me a taste of heaven in Haiti. Heavenly glimpses came with names, faces, and hugs upon arrival. Arriving in Haiti felt like going home. As new as it all was, we felt a godly assurance that God had gone before us. Before we were introduced by hands and hugs, God introduced us by heart. He had already placed us in one another's hearts by prayers and by Karris, our friend who had been living and working as a missionary at Danita's Children (www .danitaschildren.org) for more than sixteen years.

Danita, who began the center for children, has created a family. As of 2018, more than three hundred students attend her school in Ouana-minthe, Haiti, where the school's feeding program provides sixteen thousand meals each month. In eight Children's Homes, more than eighty orphaned or abandoned children live in families. Among the eighty children are twelve special needs children I consider to be my forever friends. Danita's story of going to Haiti, starting with fourteen children, and trusting that God would provide all their needs in body and spirit is one that takes your breath away. At the same time, it fills your lungs with the kind of air that makes you want to exhale the words to tell people about this haven and loving home she has made for so many hearts.

Sometimes God introduces hearts before hands, and when you meet it is as if you are already friends. I remember being embraced by these children upon arrival—hugs full and open with kindness and welcome. They already loved us; we already loved them. Our hearts knew each other, and as we began our time together praising God with worship songs in the first minutes, followed by a dance party, it was clear that this was a celebration of home, another heavenly taste of what heaven will be like. It was as though we had been missing one another all along but did not know it.

In the days that followed, I witnessed my daughter, Grace, bond with boys and girls from Haiti just because. They shared a language of play, of love, of gratitude, and of hope. She held an infant suffering from malnutrition, and I saw her look into the eyes of a toddler who was finding health for the first time. I watched Grace lift up and hold a little boy with special needs, a boy who could not move himself. A taste of heaven was happening, and I felt God smiling down.

Though Grace and I were far from our earthly address, heaven felt near and Haiti felt like home. And we could not wait to take the taste back home and share what this amazing place was doing for children in Haiti and what it had done to our hearts. We went to hold, help, and understand how we could reach the malnourished, yet we felt fed there, in a way that I had not been fed before. My brother- and sister-in-law's invitation to join was a taste of heaven.

Invite others into your joy. God multiplies it. One million meatballs! When invited, accept the invitation—and God will provide the rest.

K-Love and Moving

Sometimes God requires a smaller yes to point us to a bigger yes. He allows us the chance to practice obedience to His instruction. Zechariah 4:10 says, "Do not despise these small beginnings, for the Lord rejoices to see the work begin" (NLT).

It was not the right time. It was not the right weekend—a busy Memorial Day weekend in 2015. And I did not have the right mind-set—yet. But there was a divine invitation, and that was all I needed. I had been listening to K-Love, a Christian radio station, for a while, and quite frankly I needed it to keep my mind on heavenly things while pushing through the busy workweek.

With what could only be a gift from God, I was asked by our friend George Uribe to cohost K-Love's award show in Nashville! It did not fit easily in my schedule, but it was an invitation that felt like more. After a week of those early wake-ups, Friday would be the same—wake at 2:30 a.m. and go to work at FOX. After work, Tim and the kids picked me up, and we flew directly to Nashville from LaGuardia in time to make the night concert, a preparatory meeting for the show, and what seemed like more hosting work.

I had never cohosted an award show and did not feel "big" enough to do so. Initially, I set the invitation aside, but it did not take a side seat. It kept pressing into my heart until I said yes. It was one weekend, after all. We could do it as a family, we loved the music, and it would be something fun and different, along with learning a new skill for me. What I did not know was that God had used that small invitation to require a small yes in obedience in order to show our family something bigger. Our dearest friends, Jeannie and Mike and their boys, along with Tim's uncle John, met us in Nashville for fun and support. From bus rides to worship nights to barbecue, it was a weekend like no other.

That set of days encouraged our hearts and temporarily lifted us out of the stressful schedules we were enduring between our two careers. At a time when life was high impact, huge stress, low sleep, and intense, He gave us a Holy Spirit weekend full of praise and worship—and Him. What a gift! But that was not all. After cohosting the award show, we were so filled with the joy of it all and of the Holy Spirit that traveling home to get to work on time the next morning was unusually stress-free. Even when our flight was cancelled and then our connection was cancelled, we were actually giggling about all the travel challenges. That is how alive the Holy Spirit's joy was in us after the weekend.

I remember finally getting on a flight and asking Tim: "Do you think God wants us to move to Nashville?"

And I remember my practical-minded husband thoughtfully nodding yes as we took off.

God wanted my yes to host the award show in Nashville to take us physically to the city to give us a tiny taste of what could be. He used a small-but-not-meaningless obedient yes to plant a seed for a bigger yes.

That obedience, down the road, would require a lot. It would require stepping away from everything I had worked for in my career to step into all He wanted for me in a new season. It would require uprooting and pulling up anchors all around our life in the Northeast to make the long drive and big move as a family to Nashville.

We gave God our yes and figured out the details later. It was scary at times. It came with questions from friends and family at times. It made zero earthly sense to leave what we had and head to Tennessee. Yet all we needed was to trust. Trust and obey.

I remember telling Tim that the move had to be a drive—that I needed, and believed our family needed, to not simply "land" someplace new. I felt nudged in my heart that we had to make the long drive. We needed to see pavement rolling under us and signs change. We needed time in the transition to process, to pray, to feel the leaving, and to feel the arriving.

Obedience did not come without sadness, as we were leaving the proximity of our closest friends and family. Obedience did not feel weightless when it came to selling our home or leaving my work or saying goodbyes or packing. But through the physical obstacles and tears, the obedience came *with* the assurance of God's provision because we heard Him and said yes.

"Lord, we don't know what You have for us," we prayed, "but You are telling us to go, so it must be so. We trust You, God, with this move; we trust that You have already paved the way, and that You would not ask this of us if You did not have it ready for us."

Living in Nashville has been a meatball, a taste of heaven for us. Our friends here and church community have welcomed us with open arms and hearts. The Mondays still feel like Mondays, the homework is still homework, the flu is still the flu—but God brought us here, going before us, being with us, and surrounding us with a community that blesses us each day.

"Welcome, We Have a Spot Saved for You"

If you have ever visited the South, you know they put the *well* in *welcome.* I remember the letter from our children's new school said, "We have saved a spot for you!" A meatball it was—without a doubt—when Johnny, Saunders, and Eli were assigned to welcome our three children to Nashville as their school welcome buddies. What a taste of what God says about heaven!

They took their assignment seriously and made it an assignment of the heart—and that made our transition here feel like a soft landing. Invitations to play and swim and spend time throwing a ball around the backyard or meet for a burger or visit with their families made our kids feel the *well* in welcome. I am forever grateful to those little hearts and many more since who have jumped in and wrapped their hearts around our children's hearts! To their moms and dads—Betsy and TJ, Jody and Rob, and Ramsey and Chase—we are thankful to you for extending your homes and your hearts and for welcoming us with open arms to a new place. And in the days of decision-making, Matthew and Sarah, Tommy and Julie, and Landyn and Steve put kindness and welcome on the table, making it feel like home right away and giving us a little meatball in the South! Sometimes a taste of heaven is a southern welcome over some good food and company. Our family continues to be blessed by our new friends with awesome hearts and incredible children.

Firepit Nights, Dance Parties, and the Family Table

Whether it is a quiet night with s'mores and guitars and chairs around the fire, a Party City strobe light in the kitchen when a friend comes over, or a combination of both, I get a taste of heaven when I am with the people I love. Together is heavenly.

In the places we gather and share time together, time seems to stand still. When I am with the ones I love and we gather around the table, the island in the kitchen, or the firepit—that is where I feel close to God. When we can all hold one another's hands and see one another's eyes and lift one another's hearts, I can taste a bit of heaven. When I am with Tim, Grace, Taylor, and Isaiah, home feels like a heavenly glimpse. A roasted marshmallow becomes a meatball.

In-Betweening

"In-betweens" are those times that sneak up on you because they were neither here nor there. They are in-between your place of departure and your place of arrival, and God uses them to show you a little joy, a lot of peace, or a new face. For me, in-betweening means bus rides, road trips, walking on the beach, afternoons with nothing on the calendar, fishing on the dock, or a lazy Sunday afternoon. It means lingering to watch a sunset before dinner, waking up early to catch that sunrise, a call from a friend when you really need it, a talk with Betsy or my mom in the school pickup line because ten minutes just popped up. The in-betweens are floats in the lake with Jody, when an hour of talking knits hearts together. In-betweens are watching the children find friendships over Popsicles and lemonade stands in the front yard and that hour after they fall asleep after a day of baseball when I have my legs over Tim's lap and we get our time together. They are watching our kids fish with their uncle Nathanael on the dock in the early morning. The in-betweens are oftentimes when God gives us a meatball, a tender taste of the goodness He wants for us with one another.

I do believe that God gives us lots of chances to get a taste of heaven. And when He does, it sure does taste sweet. Thankfulness for those chances opens our eyes to see more of them as they happen. Looking for them reveals them more frequently, and that is the key to savoring more meatballs.

Nothing at All

Tim and I danced to Alison Krauss's "When You Say Nothing at All" on our wedding day. I love to dance, and Tim does not always like to dance, but whenever that song comes on, we *both* love to dance. And I love that. We have a little family fun rule that wherever we are when it comes on, we have to dance to it. A meatball set of minutes and a good reminder of how God made us for one another and continues to make us more united in those moments.

Those moments are woven together by minutes, hours, days, weeks, and years. When we dance to our song, it takes us back and reminds us of that first dance as husband and wife. Now that our children watch and wait for it, it is a reminder their little eyes love—to see us in love.

I love Mama's meatballs.

I love a taste of what is to come. The joy that comes with receiving those glimpses, those tastes of heaven, is so incredible. The joy that comes with offering a taste to someone else with kindness and welcome and invitation and warmth is full of that same joy.

Let's make some meatballs for one another every day.

Taste and see that the LORD is good; blessed
is the one who takes refuge in him.

—PSALM 34:8

Afterword

In my walk with God, I have come to trust that we have a God who wants us to see ourselves as He sees us. I believe that He wants us to take the time to peer through the lenses of influential teachers, friends, family members, and mentors who help us see things differently.

But God is not asking us to see it all. In fact, that is where faith comes in.

Faith in God requires trust and intentional practice.

Our family has a chalk wall in our house. There we write our prayers and scriptures we rely on, along with chalked and smudged doodles. When the wall is filling up and some time has passed, we have what I have named a "flashlight night."

Calling everyone to the hallway where the wall stands, I carry a tray holding some cookies or ice cream, chalk, and a flashlight. I turn the lights on, and ask, "Do you see the wall?"

They answer, "Yes."

"Is the wall there?"

"Yes, Mom."

I turn the lights off and ask, "Do you see the wall?"

"No," they say.

"Is the wall still there even when it's too dark to see it?" I ask.

"Yes."

We then take turns sitting in the dark, shining the flashlight on the words we have written. With hope about the desires of our hearts, we shine the flashlight on the prayers we can see God working on. Then when we come to the prayers that feel unanswered, we turn off the flashlight and say, "God, I don't *see* this being fixed or answered right now, but I *trust* that You are there and You are working on it."

It's kind of like how faith is. Sometimes it is bright, and we can see how God is working.

And sometimes, for days and times when it feels dark, we cannot see what He is doing.

But just as we know the wall is there even when we cannot see it, we trust that God is there even when it feels dark. We trust that He is there and He is working on it, even when we cannot see what He is doing quite yet. God is not always asking us to see it all. He does that for us.

This grown-up mom is still that little girl who smiles when things get clear. The big red glasses opened up my eyes, but the lens of God unlocked my heart.

浶

For we walk by faith, not by sight.

—2 CORINTHIANS 5:7, NKJV

Acknowledgments

In the past I have written about gluten, yet etched into my heart is the desire to write about Him. I am so grateful for the friends and family who have encouraged me throughout this process. I'm thankful for getting quiet enough to hear God's Word well.

To the most incredible team at WME, including Jim Ornstein, Mel Berger, Margaret Riley King, Jeff Lesh, and Julie Leventhal, thank you for being there for me through career changes and this entire adventure in obeying a calling. I'm not the quarterback in our house, but if I were, you would be my O-line!

To the WaterBrook team, thank you for hearing this idea in proposal form and understanding what the goal was from the jump. I am so grateful for your support and the opportunity to write about this great God! Special thanks to Susan Tjaden, my incredibly talented editor: I could not have moved these pages forward without you. Thank you for your keen eye and gift of seeing words well and for understanding my heart each day. What a joy it has been to work with you and get to know you! This entire publishing, editing, marketing, and publicity teamwork has knocked me out with gratitude. Thanks for believing in the message of this book. My appreciation and thanks also to Laura Wright, whose gift of detailed editing provided the opportunity for me to match sentence structure to the intended sentiment in each chapter. What a blessing!

Sweet and dear thanks to Beth Clark, whose careful eye and editing and writing gifts came alongside me. You took the first hard look at my words with gusto! Thank you for being so selfless and willing to work a new way—and to look at my "book board"! I am blessed by you and thankful for you! You are a woman after God's heart. When I was not sure I could write, you gave me courage!

Thank you, Jeannie Cunnion. You have been a wise and trusted friend from the start and through the pages. Thank you for your listening ear and for lighting a fire under my keyboard! See chapter 8 for more on you!

Thank you, Lauren Tomlin. Who knew a walk with you could peel away so many layers of my fear? You unraveled what was deep within. Thank you for using your gifts to point me to the yes. Thanks for hearing my heart and allowing me to process it, not as a distraction but as a sacred invitation. Thank you for unlocking my yes to this project.

Sarah Hasselbeck and Kelley Hasselbeck: In the two of you, God gave me sisters. My heart is a reflection of how much you have loved me. Running and raising children across the miles together continues to be a daily blessing. Thank you for shaping my heart. I continue to learn from, and am inspired by your hearts.

Thank you, Nathanael Hasselbeck and Matthew Hasselbeck, for being such supporters and making us smile through the years. Your brotherhood is an immeasurable gift to Tim, and to me.

To Jack and Charlie: this book will help you step up on things you cannot yet reach. One day you will write words too. Keep growing and learning. I'm blessed to be your auntie!

My thanks to Annabelle, Mallory, and Henry for your top picks for the cover and for being such bright lights. I am blessed to call you my nieces and nephew—and proud to call you friends and teammates!

Thank you, Betsy and Don Hasselbeck, for loving me like a daughter, encouraging me like a sister, and nurturing my faith walk. I'm still learning from you. You gave me a place to call home and raised the man of my dreams with the strongest heart. I am forever grateful.

To Mom, Dad, and Kenny: I'm so thankful to be your daughter and sister. By grace alone did I get to be on your team. Mom and Dad, you gave us all you had and more. I don't deserve all your sacrifice, hard work, and care. Thank you for the freedom to become who I was created to be, for the chance to go to great schools, for consistently allowing me to feel your love. Thanks for being the kind of parents I hope to be. What an awesome childhood you gave me! I can't believe I get to be your daughter every day. I get to write this story because you allowed me to grow.

Super Mimi, I stand in awe of how lovely and loving you are. I'm so blessed to be close to you, and have learned so much from you since your Timmy Tom asked me to visit Cincinnati. You are devotion and celebration, dedication, determination, poise and beauty, grace and strength personified. Your fortitude is a lighthouse for all of us, and a personal guidepost for me. It is fun to be in a Poppyseed family because of you. With all my heart, I love you.

Thank you to all our family for your examples of love and fun! May we always make meatballs like Mama and Papa and throw parades and parties like Super Mimi and Poppy.

Over the past few years, whether we were floating in a pond on a farm, walking through the park, praying on the steps, sitting near a penguin, talking on the phone, sitting in a car, sharing a spot on the bleachers, breaking bread at a table, running miles and miles, relaxing around the firepit, riding on a horse trail, talking on the back porch, hiking, sharing meals, or chatting across state borders, I have shared time with friends. My thanks to each of you. You are forever stamped in my heart because you were there, and when I shared what these pages would hold and all my hesitations, you cheered me on and lifted me up. Thank you for your wise feedback and bold prayers.

Thank you, Wiff Harmer, for the most fun photo sessions out in the open! Thank you for your artistic eye, for your natural joy, and for making me smile big for this cover and more!

Thank you, Candace, for your thoughtful words, for your faith and fellowship, for pointing our eyes to His grace each day, and for writing the words before the words of this book. I praise God for allowing our paths to cross and for us to nurture a friendship along the way. You have a "fuller house" and have filled my heart with fellowship!

Thank you, Courtney DeFeo, for your awesome eyes on the details and the big picture. Your creativity and can-do stand unmatched. I have seen your heart in action, and I'm so grateful for your input and gift of wisdom!

To Bob and sweet Maria Goff: thank you for teaching me how to communicate the gospel with ease and light and for being such wise-hearted, fun-loving, and thoughtful friends who burst *agape*. I'm forever your student.

Thank you to our nation's greatest—military members, veterans, and their families—for standing up for and protecting our freedoms. Thank you for being willing to make the ultimate sacrifice. We are free because you are brave. I stand in awe of your humility and courage. And to our friends, the Erwin family, thank you for bringing into clear focus what the gift of military service to the United States truly looks like.

A huge thank-you to Tim and kids for letting Mommy work this book out. Thank you for listening to the words that God placed in my heart and for making family memories. Grace, Taylor, and Isaiah, you would hear the words out loud and ask the best questions. It made the stories better! Keep being curious, loving, humble, giving people. Thank you, Tim, for your steady heart, your thoughtful edit, your leadership instincts, and how you care for me. I'm so well loved by you. Time with this tribe is my treasure!